Boundless Plains to Share?

Boundless Plains to Share?
Australia, Jesus, & Refugees

Scott Higgins

AJUSTCAUSE
SPEAK JUSTICE CREATE FREEDOM

ajustcause.com.au

Copyright © 2013, 2017 Scott Higgins

Title: Boundless Plains to Share? Australia, Jesus, and Refugees

Author: Scott Higgins

Edition: Third

ISBN: 978-0-9924257-8-4

ALL RIGHTS RESERVED. This book is copyright. Apart from any fair dealing for the purposes of private study, research, criticism or review, as permitted under the Copyright Act, no part of this book may be reproduced or transmitted in any form or by any means, electronic or mechanical, including photocopying, recording, or by any information storage and retrieval system without the express written permission from the author/publisher.

Scripture quotations are from the New Revised Standard Version Bible, Copyright © 1989 the Division of Christian Education of the National Council of the Churches of Christ in the United States of America. Used by permission. All rights reserved.

Contents

Introduction 1

Chapter 1 A World of Pain & Hope 3

Chapter 2 A Global Crisis 17

Chapter 3 Fortress Australia 35

Chapter 4 A Biblical Perspective 57

Chapter 5 A Better Way 75

Chapter 6 Where To From Here? 93

Bible Studies 101

Discussion Group Study 1 103

Discussion Group Study Two 107

Discussion Group Study Three 111

Discussion Group Study Four 115

Action Week 119

Introduction

Australia is a swirling mass of contradiction, fear and hope when it comes to refugees. Our status as an island nation far removed from the world's conflict hotspots means that we have very few refugees showing up on our borders seeking protection, yet we have imagined a crisis into being and enacted harsh measures to assert control over our fictional crisis. Our public discourse is characterised by half-truths, misconceptions and outright falsehoods. We have learned to fear asylum seekers and refugees. Yet there is widespread admiration for those refugees who have settled here.

Meanwhile, there is a real refugee crisis going on in the world. More than 20 million people have fled their homes and their country because it is no longer safe for them to live there. They cast themselves upon an international community that accepts responsibility to care and protect, but simply fails to deliver.

This short book is intended to help you navigate a path through the lies, distortions and half-truths to gain a sense of what is happening in the world, how it might be framed biblically, and how we might respond. We begin with the experiences of refugees, listening to their stories. From there we move to the global picture, exploring the shape of the refugee crisis and why the international protection system is failing to deliver. This gives us the necessary framework to understand Australia's place in the crisis, which we turn to in chapter 3. We trace the evolution of Australia's response to asylum seekers that arrive by boat from a stance of protecting refugees from those they are fleeing to a position of protecting ourselves from the refugees who are arriving. Having outlined the current situation and the challenges, chapter 4 explores biblical themes that should inform our response. Chapter 5 outlines what a better way forward might look like for the world and for Australia, while the final chapter provides practical suggestions as to what a local church can do to bring about change.

A four-part small group discussion guide can be found at the back of the book.

It is my hope in writing this that we will come closer to the mind and heart of God for some of the most vulnerable people on the planet.

Chapter 1
A World of Pain & Hope

"While every refugee's story is different and their anguish personal, they all share a common thread of uncommon courage: the courage not only to survive, but to persevere and rebuild their shattered lives."

Antonio Guterres
United Nations High Commissioner for Refugees

It was just a ten minute walk, but it could have been a world away. I was staying at a five-star motel in Kuala Lumpur, the capital of Malaysia. I didn't simply have a room, I had a suite, complete with lounge area, bedroom, marble floored bathroom, and kitchenette. But just ten minutes away, I found myself climbing a filthy staircase inside a crumbling tenement building. I reached the top floor and was greeted warmly but nervously by three Burmese women and their children. They were refugees, members of a persecuted ethnic minority who had fled their homeland. Their families shared this weary apartment, with its two tiny bedrooms and a makeshift third bedroom formed by a divider placed across the meagre living room. Rent was 700 Ringgit per month, too much for a single refugee family whose income averaged 800 Ringgit, but affordable if the cost was shared. I couldn't help but wonder how stressful it must be for three families to share a living space barely adequate for one.

Malaysian law prohibited refugees from working, but the authorities regularly turned a blind eye as the members of the Burmese refugee community filled low paying jobs. This of course, left the refugee workers vulnerable to exploitation. I heard multiple stories of employers who simply refused to pay wages. Who would the refugees complain to?

Healthcare was provided to refugees on a full fee paying basis. I was shown records of surgery costing 6,000 Ringgit, equivalent to more than six months wages, and far beyond the ability of any refugee to pay. To soften the blow the refugee community had developed their own rudimentary insurance scheme. Each family contributed a small amount and from the combined savings pool medical bills were paid.

Refugee children were forbidden from attending Malaysian schools. The refugee community ran its own, which I visited. One hundred children were packed into a small space while volunteers from the refugee and local Malaysian communities served as teachers.

Particularly disturbing were reports that refugees had been arrested by corrupt officials, transported to the border with Thailand, and sold into slavery. Women were sold into the Thai sex industry and men as slaves to work on Thai fishing boats.

Life in Malaysia was incredibly difficult for these refugees. Community leaders spoke of the despair felt by many of the youth, and the rise of alcohol abuse to dull the pain. What would drive people to tolerate this? The fact that life was even more difficult in their home country.

The refugees I met were Chin, one of Burma's ethnic minorities, and predominantly Christian. This brought them into conflict with the military junta that ruled Burma and used Buddhism to create a singular national identity. Systematic religious persecution followed. In 2013 an evangelist, whose pastor father had been imprisoned by the regime, arrived home to find his wife being raped by four soldiers as part of a warning to him to stop evangelising.[1] Chin religious symbols were torn down and replaced with Buddhist pagodas. The bulk of families were poor and could not afford to pay for school fees, so their only option for schooling were state sanctioned Buddhist schools in which the children were required to participate in Buddhist rituals and indoctrinated into the ways of Buddhism.

Human rights were routinely abused. A 2010 survey found that in the previous twelve months 92% of households had at least one member who was subjected to forced labour; 15% had experienced torture; 6% had household members arbitrarily detained; 5% had their home attacked or destroyed; 5% had seen a household member abducted and disappeared; 3% had a family member raped by the military.[2]

For Chin people it was only a matter of time until they were enslaved by the military, had a child tortured, their home attacked, their sister raped, their father disappeared. It is not surprising that many fled.

Cambodia

A year later I was in Cambodia, haunted by my visit to the Toul Sleng Genocide Museum and the Killing Fields. Tuol Sleng had once been a high school, but for four dark years, 1975-1979, it became the epicentre of global evil. It was here that the Khmer Rouge, headed by the maniacal Pol Pot, brought people for torture before murdering and burying them at a site that came to be known as the Killing Fields.

....

It is thought that up to 30,000 Cambodians were terrorised at Tuol Sleng. I passed interrogation rooms with single iron bedframes located in the centre. Prisoners were chained to the frames and tortured until they confessed to crimes they didn't commit. I walked into tiny cubicles where prisoners were housed – there wasn't even room to lie down. And I passed through halls where instruments and images of torture were on display, tortures I find too disturbing to describe here.

From the prison I passed to the Killing Fields. It's a place of beauty – green fields, lush trees, a warm sun and a gentle breeze. But beneath the surface of those fields lie mass graves and the remains of thousands of victims. As I walked around the site the most disturbing moment was coming across "the killing tree", where babies and infants were killed by soldiers who swung their small and fragile bodies through the air and smashed their skulls against the tree.

Theary Seng was just four years old when the Khmer Rouge swept to power. She tells her story in the book *Daughter of the Killing Field*.[3] Possessed of a bizarre vision to create a society of farmers free from technology, the regime evacuated Theary, her family, and all other residents from Phnom Penh. A short while later, Theary's father answered a call for all former civil servants to return. Theary never saw him again. He was murdered by the regime. His crime? He had worked as a civil servant for the previous regime.

Two years later, Theary, her mother, and siblings were imprisoned. At the age of seven, Theary woke one morning to discover that during the night soldiers had murdered her mother. Theary and her siblings were released, and made their way to their grandfather's village. Not long after this, the family made a long and dangerous trek to the Cambodia-Thai border. Crossing into Thailand they were finally free from the madness and the twenty years of civil war that followed Pol Pot's ousting. Theary and her family spent months in a refugee camp, before receiving the news that they had been accepted for resettlement in the United States.

Rwanda

In 1991 Muhumaad Saeed left his home country, Rwanda, to study in Pakistan, but by the time he finished university three years later, his nation was caught up in one of the bloodiest conflicts of the modern era. In one hundred days of madness, over half a million Tutsis were murdered, including two of Muhamaad's siblings.

The horror of the situation in Muhamaad's homeland was captured by Bishop John Ruchyahana in his book *The Bishop of Rwanda*.[4]

> There was a loud cracking sound, and the door to the hut shattered in pieces. Several men carrying machetes and clubs stood grinning hideously in the torchlight. One of them stepped inside. It was Ndanguza, their neighbour from up the hill...

There were several men inside their hut now, moving towards Peter. He stood up and held out his hands to plead with them...One of the men brought his machete down hard on Peter's outstretched arm, nearly hacking off his hand at the wrist. [His wife] Sefa screamed, but then three men grabbed her and threw her down on the bed. They began tearing off her clothes. She saw two other men attack her boys while the others chopped at Peter as he lay bleeding on the floor of the hut. Two men held Sefa while a third raped her. She tried to hold on to the baby, but another man came and took him by his feet...She stared at her oldest son's severed foot lying on the ground; she couldn't see the rest of him. As the men changed positions and a second man was on top of her, she looked at her husband. There was blood everywhere, and he was twisted in a strange position. Then she realised that his head had been chopped off...

Then out of the corner of her eye she saw a torch. They were setting fire to the hut...and to Sefa's horror they lit the baby on fire...

It was such violence and a fear of its return that meant Muhamaad spent the next twenty years in Pakistan as a refugee. He married a Rwandan woman, Aliya, also made a refugee by the crisis. For two decades it remained unsafe for them to return home, but they never abandoned the dream. In January 2013 they became the first Rwandans repatriated from Pakistan under the United Nations High Commission on Refugees voluntary repatriation program.[5]

The Democratic Republic of Congo

Scisa Rumenge was at a church choir meeting when his village was attacked. He returned home to find the charred bodies of his father, mother, brother and sister among the smoldering remains of what had been his village. Scisa fled to another part of the country only to be imprisoned and repeatedly beaten by an armed militia after he refused to join them. Scisa was a victim of war in his homeland, the Democratic Republic of Congo.

> The infamous Ituri conflict – the "war within the war" – erupted in 1999 at the height of the Second Congo war. External factors, such as Ituri's occupation by Ugandan forces, came into play, but violence emerged primarily from a struggle to control land by the Lendu and Hema, two of the region's dominant ethnic groups. The war was fought between consortiums of local tribal militias and proxies in the form of Ugandan, Rwandan, and Congolese armies. Disorganised bands, often armed only with machetes, clubs, lances and bows and arrows descended on civilian populations, killing, raping, and burning as they went. Victims, including women and children, were often brutally mutilated. Grisly photos of young men proudly posing next to neat rows of severed heads circulated among humanitarian workers.[6]

Scisa escaped and made his way to Kenya, where he was recognised as a refugee and sent to the Kakuma refugee camp. He joined tens of thousands of victims of violence from eleven nations seeking to construct something new out of life. Conditions were harsh. Refugees were not allowed to seek work outside the camp, which made them dependent on provisioning from the World Food Program (WFP). The WFP was however so chronically underfunded that it could not deliver the recommended caloric intake for refugees. Violence was common. Incidents involving death and serious injury occurred daily.[7]

Yet amid such pain and trauma, it was the kindness of another refugee family that helped Scisa's healing process begin. In Kakuma he felt very alone and afraid, until a Somali family invited Scisa to live with them and embraced him as an adopted son. Scisa spent five years in Kakuma before being resettled to the United States in 2011, where he went on to study film and begin a new life.[8]

Vietnam

Ahn Do is a popular Australian comedian. In 2010 he released a book, *The Happiest Refugee,* that describes his life as a refugee from Vietnam. His uncles fought against the Communist regime that, once it won the war, sent them to a concentration camp to be "re-educated". For three years they suffered hunger, violence, and disease. A number of their fellow prisoners died from sickness, starvation, or execution. Ahn's father engaged in a daring rescue. He got hold of a high ranking military officer's uniform, walked into the prison, demanded Ahn's uncles be released to him, and walked out with them by his side. After this, the family had to flee. They sold everything they owned to purchase a nine metre fishing boat, which they would use to make their way to Malaysia.

Narrowly escaping the Vietnamese navy, everyone's spirits were lifted when, after days at sea, a fishing vessel spotted them. Hope turned to horror. The fishing vessel was crewed by pirates who stole their supplies of food and drink, their jewellery, and their engine. A second motor, overlooked by the pirates, was stolen when a second group of pirates attacked. Adrift at sea, with precious little water and no motor, despair set in. It turned into joy when a German ship found the band of sunburnt, weakened refugees and took them to Malaysia.

After three months in a Malaysian refugee camp the family was offered the opportunity to settle in Australia. Here they began a new life.

The journey from Vietnam to Malaysia was also taken by Hiue and Lan Van Le. They were a newly married couple when the Communists won the Vietnam War. For those in the south this inaugurated a period of fear, loss of freedom, and violence. 65,000 Vietnamese were executed and a million were sent to concentration camps. In 1977 Hiue and Lan reluctantly reached the conclusion that they had to leave their country if they were to be safe.

A fisherman offered to smuggle them and a group of others out of the country. When they reached the open sea they learned, to their horror, that the fishermen had no experience offshore. Hiue drew a rough map and they navigated their way across the ocean, hoping to land in either Thailand or Malaysia. They just wanted to get somewhere they could be safe and free.

When they arrived off the coast of Malaysia they discovered there was no welcome for them. On nine occasions they were met by the coastguard and pushed away, often down the barrel of a gun. They became so desperate that on their ninth attempt to land they got close to shore, jumped overboard and swam past the coastguard.

Life in Malaysia was miserable. Hiue and Lan were stuck inside a refugee camp that was overcrowded and rife with disease and hunger. Nor was any other country in the world offering to take them. Hiue and Lan were filled with despair. The future looked like years, decades even, inside a refugee camp. So they made a decision they would make another boat trip, this time to Australia where they knew they would find freedom. It was a dangerous and difficult journey, but after a month at sea they eventually arrived in Darwin Harbour. As dawn approached they heard the gurgling of an outboard motor and instantly they were frightened. Surely this was the coastguard coming to push them back out to sea? It was in fact two fishermen in a tinny. They manoeuvred close to the refugee boat, held up a beer can, and shouted "Gday mates. Welcome to Australia."

In 2011 Hiue gave a speech at Old Parliament House in which he reflected on that moment:

> We were stunned by the warmth and good nature of this laconic welcome. And that one moment in time has left a lifelong impression on me.
>
> My personal navigation to Australia had been a combination of dark circumstance, accident, fear, despair, but most of all, of hope.
>
> Like most other migrants and refugees, I arrived on this silver shore with nothing but my invisible suitcase of cultural heritage and dreams.
>
> At another time, another place, a traveller such as me might have been greeted with fear or hostility. But at that time, in this place, I was given the unfettered wish and opportunity to show gratitude.
>
> What greeted me was a remarkable generosity of spirit.[9]

In 2014 Hiue became the Governor of South Australia.

20 Million Stories

There are more than 20 million refugees in the world today and they each have a story to tell. The names and locations differ, but they all share a common theme: persecution in their homeland forced them to flee.

The public discourse around refugees would be different if we began by listening to their stories. Stories bring us down out of the clouds of abstraction, ideology, mythology, and politicking to the realities of life. Listen to stories like those told in this chapter and it becomes impossible to demonise refugees and asylum seekers. Rather, we are driven to empathy and compassion for people whose reality is tinged with pain, trauma, and hope of a safe future.

Chapter 2
A Global Crisis

"People are dying and they need our help. If we cannot see that, then we have no right to look away from the consequences of inaction."

The Independent, September 2015

At the end of 2015 there were 65.3 million people across the world who had been forcibly displaced from their homes. Of these, 21.3 million were refugees and 3.2 million were asylum seekers.[10] They lived in countries that were not their own, one-third inside camps and two-thirds in private accommodation within villages, towns and cities.[11] Over 50% were children. Many experienced ongoing violations of their most basic human rights and struggled to meet their most basic human needs. They had thrown themselves upon the international community and its promise to offer them protection, only to find that community struggling to make good on its pledge.

As long as we live in a world in which States use violence against their citizens, it will be a world that includes people who flee their homeland in search of safety. The international community has accepted that when this occurs, it has a responsibility to offer protection. Shortly after World War II it developed the apparatus by which it would do so, and this continues to guide the response to refugees today. When it works as it should, the protection system is life-giving, sheltering people from horrific violence and providing an opportunity to rebuild their lives. All too often however, the protection system fails them, leaving refugees in situations where they face years, even decades, living a shadowy existence as non-citizens in States that are either unable or unwilling to respect their rights and an international community that is unwilling to equitably share responsibility for their protection.

The International Protection System

The foundation of the international protection system is the Convention Relating to the Status of Refugees, adopted in 1951 to guide the global response to refugees created by World War II and in 1967 extended to apply to refugees everywhere. The Convention lays out the rights and responsibilities of both refugees and the nations to which they flee, and the need for a cooperative international community to share the responsibility of providing protection.

Who is a Refugee?

The Convention defines a refugee as someone who

> "owing to a well-founded fear of being persecuted for reasons of race, religion, nationality, membership of a particular social group or political opinion, is outside the country of his nationality and is unable, or owing to such fear, is unwilling to avail himself of the protection of that country; or who, not having a nationality and being outside the country of his or her habitual residence, is unable, or, owing to such fear, is unwilling to return to it."

In other words, a refugee is not someone who migrates to another country for economic or lifestyle reasons, but someone who flees their country because they have been persecuted, or would be persecuted if they returned. They may be rich or poor; highly educated or with few formal educational qualifications; Christian,

Muslim, Buddhist, Hindu, Jewish, or of no faith. They are united by one thing – the experience of persecution.

Every refugee is first an asylum seeker. They have fled their homeland and asked another country for protection, but their claim that they cannot return home for fear of persecution needs to be tested. As long as their claim is untested they are referred to as "asylum seekers". If their claim is found to be unproven they are not considered refugees and are not able to access the provisions of the Convention. If however it is found that they cannot return home due to a well-grounded fear of persecution they are classified as refugees and have a right to access all the Convention provisions.

Key Principles

The Convention is grounded on four key principles:

1. **Non-discrimination.** Refugees are to be provided with protection without discrimination based on race, religion, or country of origin. To these grounds we now commonly add discrimination based on sex, age, disability, or sexuality;
2. **Non-penalisation.** Refugees are not to be penalised for the manner of their arrival in a country. Nations maintain control over their borders by requiring anybody who is not a citizen to gain permission to enter. This is usually done through the granting of visas. The Convention recognises, however, that those fleeing persecution are rarely able to avail themselves of formal migratory channels. For this reason, refugees

are not to be penalised for arriving in a country in a manner outside the law;
3. ***Non-refoulement.*** This prohibits refugees being returned against their will to the country they have fled or to any other country where the refugee fears a threat to life or freedom;
4. **Minimum Standards.** Refugees are to enjoy the freedoms necessary to establish a decent life. The Convention specifically mentions areas such as freedom of movement; access to education; access to health care; access to the courts; and the right to work.

Durable Solutions

Since the Convention was adopted the international community has recognised that there are three ways a refugee might construct a safe future. First, refugees may return home if and when they are convinced it is safe for them to do so. Second, they may integrate into the life of the country in which they have found asylum. To be integrated means they are treated like any other resident of the country, sharing the same rights and responsibilities and making their country of asylum their home. Third, they may be resettled in another country.

International Cooperation

The preamble to the Convention recognises

> that the grant of asylum may place unduly heavy burdens on certain countries, and that a satisfactory solution of a problem of which the United Nations has

recognized the international scope and nature cannot therefore be achieved without international co-operation.

This recognises that refugee flows are uneven, rapid and unpredictable. Between 2011 and 2016, for example, over 5 million Syrians fled their homeland. The vast majority fled to the countries with which Syria shares a border – Jordan, Turkey, and Lebanon. In a very short period of time these nations found themselves struggling to provide services to large refugee populations – more than 600,000 in Jordan, 1 million in Lebanon, and 2 million in Turkey. In circumstances like these, protection requires other members of the international community to provide material support to host nations and to resettle large numbers of their refugees.

Unequal Burden Sharing

Many people assume that the bulk of the world's refugees and asylum seekers are found in wealthy, industrialised countries. The reality is that developing countries assume the vast burden of providing protection. In 2015, for example, developing countries were host to 86% of the world's refugees.[14] Not a single western nation was found in the top 10 host countries ranked according to the number of refugees they hosted.

TOP 10 HOST COUNTRIES FOR REFUGEES END 2015 (excluding Palestinian refugees)	
1. Turkey	2,541,352
2. Pakistan	1,561,162
3. Lebanon	1,070,854
4. Iran	979,437
5. Ethiopia	750,086
6. Jordan	664,118
7. Kenya	553,912
8. Uganda	511,936
9. DR Congo	477,187
10. Chad	369,540

Source: UNHCR Global Trends 2015

If we expand our view to countries with relatively large refugee populations, in 2015 23 countries hosted over 200,000 refugee or asylum seekers. Of the 23, only three were highly developed countries, but nine were among the least developed.

The reason for this is simple. Refugees flee to neighbouring countries and usually wait there until it is safe to return home. The countries that host the greatest number of refugees therefore are usually those that share a border with the countries that are the main sources of refugees. For example, 88% of refugees from Syria have

REFUGEE HOST COUNTRIES BY DEVELOPMENT STATUS

COUNTRIES HOSTING MORE THAN 200,000 REFUGEES AT END 2015	
Development status (UNHDI 2015)	Country
Very high	Germany, USA, France
High	Turkey, Lebanon, Iran, Jordan, China, Russia,
Medium	Congo, Iraq, Bangladesh, Egypt, India
Low	Pakistan, Kenya, Ethiopia, Chad, Cameroon, Sudan, Yemen, South Sudan, Afghanistan

SOURCES: UNHCR Mod Year Statistical Review 2015; UN Human Development Index 2015

made their way to the neighbouring states of Turkey, Jordan and Lebanon.[15]

This can impose substantial challenges on the host country. It is the nature of refugee movements that they occur unexpectedly and often involve large numbers of people shifting very rapidly from their home state to a state of asylum. Demand on services such as education, housing, infrastructure, and healthcare grows, but the country may not have the capacity to grow them at the pace required. The additional demand may well drive up the price of food and rents but may have the opposite effect upon wages in those industries in which refugees seek work.[16]

The Syrian civil war, for example, created massive refugee flows into Lebanon. Between 2011 and 2016 over

1 million refugees poured into this nation of just 4.8 million people. This placed enormous pressure on local infrastructure and services. Prior to the Syrian crisis there were 300,000 children in Lebanese public schools. By 2016 an additional 395,000 Syrian children were in the system, more than doubling the demand for teachers, school infrastructure and funding, something that was beyond the capacity of the state to meet.[17] The World Bank estimated that, because of the Syrian crisis, 200,000 Lebanese fell into poverty between 2011 and 2016, and that an additional 250,000-300,000 Lebanese citizens became unemployed. Annual GDP growth, which had been running at above 8% pa from 2007-2010, fell below 2% pa from 2014-2016, impacted not only by the cost of the massive influx of refugees but also by the loss of trade with a now war-torn neighbour.[18]

Or consider the 2015 spike in refugee flows across the Mediterranean to Europe. Prior to the Syrian crisis, Europe received relatively small numbers of refugees and migrants crossing from north Africa and had systems in place to manage them. In 2014 the Syrian crisis spilled beyond the Middle Eastern nations and began to be felt in Europe. At the peak, more than 1,000,000 people arrived, some claiming asylum, others simply migrants in search of a better life.

There is no doubt that Europe was much better placed to receive a million refugees than a country like Lebanon, and in the long-term there may be benefits. The populations of most Western countries are ageing, and refugees, who tend to be younger than the general population, may well contribute to the viability of European economies. Yet in the short term, there are challenges to face in ensuring a sudden and substantial surge in the provision of housing, schooling, nutrition, and gainful employment.[19]

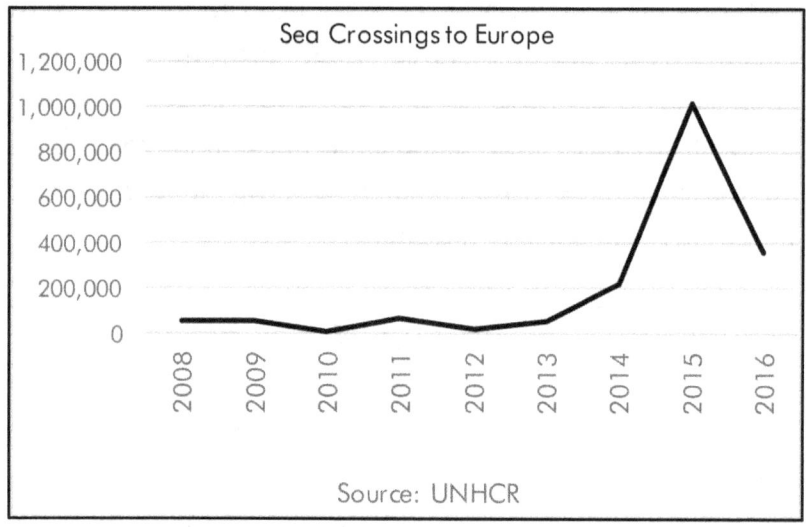

Refugee flows will always be unevenly distributed among the countries of the world, so it is incumbent on the international community to ensure that nations with large refugee flows receive the support they need to provide protection. They can do this by direct assistance and by supporting agencies such as the UNHCR and the World Food Program. Yet the funding is inadequate. For example, each year from 2011-2015, the UNHCR raised only 50-60% of its required budget. UNHCR's budget shortfall for 2015 was $3.574 billion, which meant 1.5 million people were unable to be provided with shelter; 963,000 people were unable to be provided with cash and voucher assistance; 1.1 million people were unable to receive winter support; 7.1 million people were unable to receive core relief items; 905,000 children were unable to receive education support; and 2.1 million women were unable to be provided with sanitary materials.[20] Moreover, 85% of funds were earmarked by donors, mainly governments, for specific purposes. This meant that in 2015, UNHCR's Special Mediterranean Initiative, which had high support from European nations, received 100% of the funds required, while UNHCR's work in the Central African Republic received just 24% of the funds required.

Violations of Convention Principles

Although the Refugee Convention requires refugees to be given access to the resources they need to sustain a decent life, the reality is commonly far short of this. Some host nations are not signatories to the Refugee Convention, others are but ignore parts of it, while others are simply overwhelmed by their massive refugee populations and unable to provide the care refugees require.

For example, in 2012 the Dadaab Refugee Camp in Kenya held more than 465,000 refugees, and had existed for more than 20 years in "an almost perpetual humanitarian crisis"[21]. In two of the most populated areas 58,000 refugees did not have access to adequate health care. Health posts were inadequate, overcrowded, understaffed and underequipped; there was a lack of nutrition nurses to provide 24-hour care for an average of 60 severely malnourished children with medical complications each month; a lack of community health workers to manage disease outbreaks and identify malnourished children; no water and sanitation services to 50,000 refugees; 130,000 refugees were without adequate shelter; 164,000, or 70%, of children were out of school; 20% of refugee households faced threats, harassment and discrimination; there was a 36% increase in reports of sexual violence, but inadequate services to meet the needs of survivors; thousands of children lacked access to any child protection support.

A 2015 World Bank study found that

> Syrian refugees in Jordan and Lebanon live in precarious circumstances. Although many Syrians are registered as refugees with the UNHCR and the authorities, this does not confer legal rights or entitlements for assistance. The majority of refugees in both countries live on the margins, in urban and peri-urban areas, many in informal settlements. Their access to government services is severely constrained by supply shortages generated by the enormous increase in demand. Only a minority are housed in refugee camps, where most of their essential

material needs are met and financed by the international community. [22]

Alongside Jordan and Lebanon, Turkey has also received large refugee flows from the Syrian war. In the space of just five years from 2011-2016, 2.5 million Syrian refugees crossed the border into Turkey. It was initially believed that the civil war would end quickly and the refugees were received as "guests" not "refugees". The conditions in Syria didn't change and hundreds of thousands of refugees began pouring into Turkey. The country's refugee camps could hold around 200,000 people, so most refugees lived in private accommodation in cities or on the streets. Less than 0.5% were granted work permits, leaving Syrian refugees working illegally or informally and at the mercy of unscrupulous employers.

A Syrian mathematics teacher named Ali, who arrived in Istanbul with his two sons and his life savings of USD $6,000, described his circumstances to Al-Monitor

> I am a math teacher with 20 years of experience, but none of the Syrian schools in Istanbul want to hire me.

The only employment he could find was in a sweat shop, sewing clothes. He worked 11-hour days, six days a week and earned 1,000 Turkish lira (about AUS $390) per month. This covered his rent and utilities and nothing more. His sons, aged 12 and 14, were not in school but worked in in the sweatshop for about half the money their father earned.

Eighteen months after arriving in Turkey Ali's life savings had been reduced to 50 lira. He commented that "I don't want to be rich, but I've lost hope."[23]

Lack of Durable Solutions

The international protection system identifies three durable solutions for refugees: voluntary return home when it is safe to do so; integration into the host nation; or resettlement in a third country. Unfortunately, in any given year only a fraction of the world's refugees are able to access these solutions. In 2015, for example, 201,400 refugees returned to their home country. This represented less than 1% of the global refugee population.[24] Some years the figure is higher. In 2005 5.3% of refugees returned home, but this was exceptional.[25] From 2009-2014 the annual average was just 0.9%.[26] For the other 99.1% their home country remained unsafe.

It is difficult to accurately estimate the number of refugees who integrate, for this is usually a slow and informal process in which refugees are accepted as members of the local community with the same opportunities as locals. The UNHCR estimates that over the course of the decade to 2016 1.1 million refugees became citizens of the countries in which they found asylum.[27] In 2015 only 32,000, or 0.15%, of the world's refugees were naturalised.[28]

Resettlement numbers are much clearer, with around 80,000-110,000 places made available each year. In

2015 107,100, or 0.5% of the world refugees, were resettled in one of thirty-three countries.[29] The United States resettled 82,500 refugees, followed by Canada with 22,900 and Australia resettling 9,300.[30]

GLOBAL REFUGEE RESETTLEMENT NEEDS		
YEAR	NEED	RESETTLED
2011	805,500	61,649
2012	781,299	69,252
2013	859,300	71,411
2014	691,000	73,608
2015	960,000	81,893
2016	1,150,000	
2017	1,190,000	

SOURCE: UNHCR, GLOBAL RESETTLEMENT NEEDS REPORTS

Each year the UNHCR recommends people for resettlement, selecting refugees who are most vulnerable and cannot wait for years for another option to open up. The UNHCR list is comprised of women and girls who are at risk; children and youth at risk, refugees with medical needs, survivors of torture and violence; those without any foreseeable alternative durable solution; and some with family reunion needs. The need vastly outstrips the availability of places. In any given year, less than 10% of those needing resettlement find it.

Voluntary return when it is safe, integration and resettlement represent positive futures for refugees. But these futures are shut off to most. In 2015 more than 98% of the world's refugees had no durable solution but were living as marginalised people in countries that were not their own. Rather than working together to create a durable solution for every refugee, countries around the world are shifting their focus from protection to deterrence through measures such as closing their borders to refugees or by violating the Convention rights of refugees.

The absence of durable solutions means the global refugee crisis is only going to grow worse as the number of new refugees each year exceeds the number of those finding solutions. In 2015, for example, there were 1.8 million new refugees and 2 million new asylum seekers[31], yet only 340,000 refugees accessed a durable solution.

Some Conclusions

The world faces a refugee crisis but the absence of commitment to equitable burden-sharing means the international protection system is breaking down. The bulk of the world's refugees live in difficult circumstances, having found asylum in countries where their human rights are not respected or where the sheer weight of numbers are beyond the capacity of poor country governments to provide adequate services. At the same time the response of the industrialised nations has been thoroughly inadequate. They have failed to ensure host nations and the international bodies such as UNHCR are adequately funded and accept for resettlement only a fraction of those who need it.

Chapter 3
Fortress Australia

"We will decide who comes to this country and the circumstances under which they come."

John Howard
Twenty-Fifth Prime Minister of Australia

In 2001 a Norwegian cargo ship, *The Tampa*, responded to a distress signal from a boat 140 kilometres north of Christmas Island carrying asylum seekers on their way to Australia. An election campaign was under way in Australia and the predicament of these "boat people" ignited public debate. Prime Minister Howard ordered the captain of *The Tampa* to take the asylum seekers to Indonesia. The nearest port was found there and the asylum seekers had been rescued within the area for which Indonesia had search and rescue responsibilities. Yet when the captain turned the ship, the 438 people he had rescued became very agitated. Fearing a riot, or that his passengers would make good on a threat to throw themselves overboard, he set sail for Christmas Island, creating a tense stand-off with the Australian Government. Australia threatened to have the captain charged with people-smuggling, sent the Navy to board and redirect the ship, and passed legislation to exclude Christmas Island from Australia's migration zone, which allowed the asylum seekers to be transferred to Nauru. During this episode, Prime Minister Howard famously declared his foundational principle: "We will decide who comes to this country and the circumstances under which they come."

In a world in which the number of refugees is large and growing, Australia's status as an island nation that is distant and difficult to reach means only a very small proportion of the world's asylum seekers have arrived on our shores. Between 2009 and 2013, for example, Australia received just 3% of asylum applications made to industrialised countries.[38] In 2013 Australia received its largest number of asylum applications (24,320), yet they still constituted only 3.9% of asylum applications to industrialised countries. If every applicant had been found to be a refugee and offered protection, they would have constituted just 0.1% of our population.

The first boats of asylum seekers arrived from Vietnam in 1976. At first there was little discussion in the press and the passengers were granted protection visas.[39] This changed as more boats arrived. Questions were raised about the bona fides of the refugees and fears were expressed that, if not managed properly, the trickle of boats would turn into a flood. Ted Robertson, Labor Senator for the Northern Territory, talked about the need to "find a way of showing our sympathy while stopping the flood of what are basically illegal immigrants."[40] The Minister for Immigration, Michael Mackellar gave a speech in which he argued that

> No country can afford the impression that any group of people who arrive on its shores will be allowed to enter and remain...We have to combine humanity and compassion with prudent control of unauthorised entry, or be prepared to tear up the Migration Act and its basic policies.[41]

Growing anxiety about asylum seekers arriving by boat saw Australia's policy shift from one in which we sought to protect boat arrivals to one in which we penalised them. Indeed, many Australians felt it was

Australia that needed to be protected from asylum seekers.

In 1992 the Keating government introduced indefinite mandatory detention for all who arrived in Australia without approved travel documents, which included all boat arrivals. Other nations detain asylum seekers temporarily so that health and criminality checks can be carried out and then release them into the community where they can start building a new life while their application for refugee status is processed. The Keating Government policy meant asylum seekers arriving by boat would be held in prison-like conditions for the entire period during which their asylum claims were processed. Gerry Hand, then Minister for Immigration, spelled out the reason when introducing the legislation:

> The Government is determined that a clear signal be sent that migration to Australia may not be achieved by simply arriving in this country and expecting to be allowed into the community.[42]

The Refugee Convention guarantees those fleeing persecution the right to enter a country without approval, seek asylum, and not be punished for doing so. The introduction of mandatory and indefinite detention saw Australia walk away from this obligation. Asylum seekers arriving by boat were now to be treated harshly in order to persuade others who might follow that the trip was not worthwhile.

Australia alone practises indefinite mandatory detention.[43] Refugee advocates decried the policy as a violation of the Refugee Convention and medical practitioners pointed to the psychological damage lengthy detention inflicts.[44] Despite such protestations, the policy has been continued by successive governments. Psychiatrist Patrick McGorry, appointed 2010 Australian of the Year in recognition of his work in mental illness among young people, described detention centres as "factories for producing mental illness and mental disorder".[45] Indeed, given the people most likely to arrive in Australia without visas are those who are fleeing extreme violence and dysfunctional government,

> The cruel irony is that instead of providing special care for the most traumatised individuals fleeing persecution, western countries may be subjecting them to the very conditions that are likely to hinder psychosocial recovery.[46]

Yet despite the mandatory detention policy, boats filled with asylum seekers continued to arrive. This led successive governments to implement additional deterrent measures. The Howard government introduced temporary protection visas (TPVs) for refugees who arrived by boat. Every three years their status would be reassessed, and if things had improved in their home country, they would be sent back. As long as they held a TPV they could not re-enter Australia should they leave, nor would family members overseas be eligible to migrate to Australia. Psychologists once again warned of the debilitating psychological impacts that TPVs had on highly traumatised people. TPVs meant boat arrivals were unable to live with any certainty about their future and thus unable to build a new life. The Kaldor Centre for International Refugee Law notes that

> A study by mental health experts in 2006 found that refugees on TPVs experienced higher levels of anxiety, depression and post-traumatic stress disorder than refugees on permanent PVs, even though both groups of refugees had experienced similar levels of past trauma and persecution in their home countries.[47]

In a further effort to prevent people from arriving by boat, the Howard government excised Christmas, Ashmore, Cartier and Cocos (Keeling) Islands from the Australian migration zone. These islands, located north-west of the mainland, were places boats carrying asylum seekers commonly landed. Once excised, asylum seekers landing there need not be treated as though they had landed in Australia. Rather, Nauru and Papua New Guinea agreed to take them. They would not have access to the Australian courts, nor be guaranteed resettlement in Australia.

The Rudd government abandoned the "Pacific solution" and temporary protection visas, only to implement even harder measures after a refugee boat broke up on rocks off Christmas Island in 2010. Fifty asylum seekers drowned and the danger of their trip was horrifically played out in full public view. The political rhetoric switched from the importance of controlling our borders to the need to deter people from risking their lives at sea.

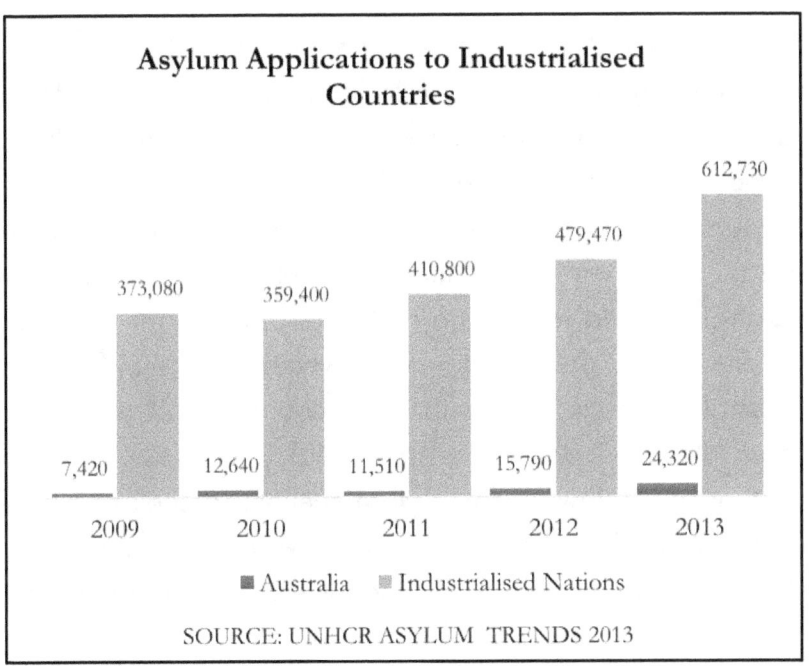

In 2012 and 2013 the number of people arriving by boat spiked sharply, from 4,565 in 2011 to 17,204 in 2012 and 20,587 in 2013. This translated into a peak of 24,320 asylum applications in 2013. Given Australia's low number of boat arrivals in the past, the spike created the impression that suddenly we were taking large numbers of asylum seekers. Yet the same year Australia had 24,320 asylum applications, Germany had 101,980; France 60,100; Turkey 55,810; Sweden 54,260; and the US 88,360.[48]

The spike triggered a fierce debate. Was this surge driven by factors outside Australia's control or had the Rudd government suddenly made Australia an attractive destination that incentivised people to seek us out?

In 2012 an expert panel was tasked with determining a way for Australia to prevent boats from arriving. The panel made two key recommendations. First, a policy of "no advantage" should be applied. To deter asylum seekers from arriving by boat it should be made clear that their application for refugee protection in Australia would receive no higher priority than if they had applied from the country from which they left. Second, Australia should work with other countries in the region, particularly Indonesia and Malaysia, to develop authorised pathways for asylum seekers to seek and find protection. The Rudd-Gillard government, then the Coalition governments that followed, would implement the first measure but not the second.

Agreements were reached with the governments of Nauru and Papua New Guinea that saw detention centres established on Nauru and Manus Island. Any asylum seeker arriving by boat after July 19, 2013 was sent to one of these detention facilities. Not only would a no advantage test apply, but it was legislated that they would not be permitted to resettle in Australia.

The policy however came at a heavy price. Greg Lake, who served as Director of Offshore Processing and Transfers during this period, described the approach as the deliberate and intentional removal of hope. Take away a person's hope and they no longer have the will to live. ... As many asylum seekers flee countries, which are so dangerous that [death] is a very real and present fear, the only other way to create a meaningful deterrent in practice, is to actively remove a person's sense of hope. The intention is that these hopeless, broken people then send a message back to any family members or friends who might be in transit towards Australia that it isn't worth coming.[49]

This conclusion was shared by others. In July 2014, Dr Peter Young, who had spent three years as Director of Mental Health for International Health and Medical Services, the organisation appointed by the government to oversee health care in detention centres, argued that detainees were intentionally harmed in an effort to convince them to return to their home country.[50]

Jane McAdam, Scientia Professor of Law and Director of the Kaldor Centre for International Refugee Law at UNSW, and Fiona Chong, a former research assistant to Professor McAdam, comment that

> ...all the major UN human rights bodies have condemned Australia's system of mandatory detention as a violation of Article 9 of the International Covenant on Civil and Political Rights...
>
> In the international community there is both dismay and bewilderment at Australia's treatment of refugees and asylum seekers. International institutions, such as the

> United Nations High Commissioner for Refugees and the Office of the United Nations Commissioner for Human Rights, as well as a number of the United Nation's expert Special Rapporteurs, continue to highlight how Australian practises breach international treaties and place individuals at risk. This is damaging Australia's reputation as a good international citizen.[51]

Reports by Amnesty International, the United Nations High Commissioner for Refugees, the Australian Human Rights Commission, and the government's own Moss Review highlighted violations of human rights and dignity in Australia's offshore detention centres.[52]

Despite the damage to asylum seekers and the opprobrium of the international community, the deterrence approach was further enhanced when the Abbott government reintroduced TPVs and rigorously applied a policy of boat turn backs. Boats carrying asylum seekers would be intercepted by the Australian Navy and sent back to the port from which they had set out. Australia even purchased emergency life rafts, and used them to return asylum seekers if their boat was unseaworthy. Between December 2013 and September 2016 29 boats carrying more than 740 asylum seekers were turned around.[53] In the three years following the implementation of the turn-back policy the arrival of boats to Australia was effectively halted.

With these measures in place Australia's policy of deterrence rather than protection had finally succeeded.

Creating the Myths That Justify Deterrence

Australians like to see themselves as a fair and compassionate people, so it was inevitable that myths would be generated to justify the harsh treatment of asylum seekers who arrived by boat. Who wants to admit that they're locking up innocent people, stripping them of their rights, and driving them to despair? Five myths have proven particularly strong.

The Lesser of Two Evils Myth

The International Office of Migration estimates that from 2000-2014 1495 people died trying to get to Australia, most on board boats that set out from Indonesia.[54] The lesser of two evils myth argues that the harsh deterrent measures Australia imposed were necessary to prevent people from drowning at sea, the victims of unscrupulous people smugglers. While a Minister in the Abbot government, future Prime Minister Malcolm Turnbull expressed it like this:

> Our policy is a harsh one, it really is. All of the policies to deal with asylum seekers and people smuggling are harsh, cruel in fact. But the problem is the status quo is cruel. It is analogous to what people say about the Middle East: there is no shortage of bad options here. You have to work out the least cruel, most effective, most efficient means of depriving the people smuggler of a product to sell.[55]

There are two problems with this argument. The first is that it is highly questionable that the policy achieves the aim of preventing deaths. People board boats because they are desperate. Having fled persecution in their home country, they find themselves in difficult circumstances in the country to which they fled, have very little prospect of returning home, integrating where they are, or being resettled in a third country. By closing off access to Australia we simply reduce by one the number of countries to which they can seek entry. For example, Hazara's coming from South Asia, where their lives are under threat, typically fly to Malaysia, take a boat or plane to Indonesia, then set out from Indonesia in a boat to Australia. In both Indonesia and Malaysia life is difficult. Without work rights, welfare, access to the health system, and the ever present threat of incarceration, they subsist in poverty and danger. So what will they do now the route to Australia is shut? They will still flee persecution in Afghanistan and Pakistan, but will journey somewhere else. That journey will inevitably involve being smuggled into countries, which almost everywhere in the world is dangerous.

The second problem with the lesser of two evils argument is that it only works if there are but two options: offshore detention or people drowning. Yet there are a number of ways Australia could stop people drowning at sea without resorting to cruelty. For example, rather than deploying the Navy to intercept asylum boats and turn them around, the Navy could escort boats safely to

Australia. Similarly, a partnership with the Indonesian Government to establish a centre in Indonesia that processes asylum claims quickly and to share responsibility for settling those found to be refugees would eliminate the incentive for people to board boats.

The Undeserving Refugee Myth

A second myth asserts that refugees coming to Australia by boat are undeserving. This myth has several versions:

1. Those coming by boat are not "genuine refugees";
2. Those coming by boat are "queue jumpers" who unfairly take the places of refugees who have waited patiently in a camp overseas;
3. Those coming by boat are "illegals".

These claims are simply untrue. First, the vast majority of those who have arrived by boat were found to be refugees. As noted earlier, asylum seekers can come to Australia on a visa, such as student or tourist visa, and apply for protection once here, or they can arrive by boat without a visa. Of those who arrive with a visa around 45-50% have historically been found to be refugees. Yet among those who come by boat 88-100% have historically been found to be refugees.

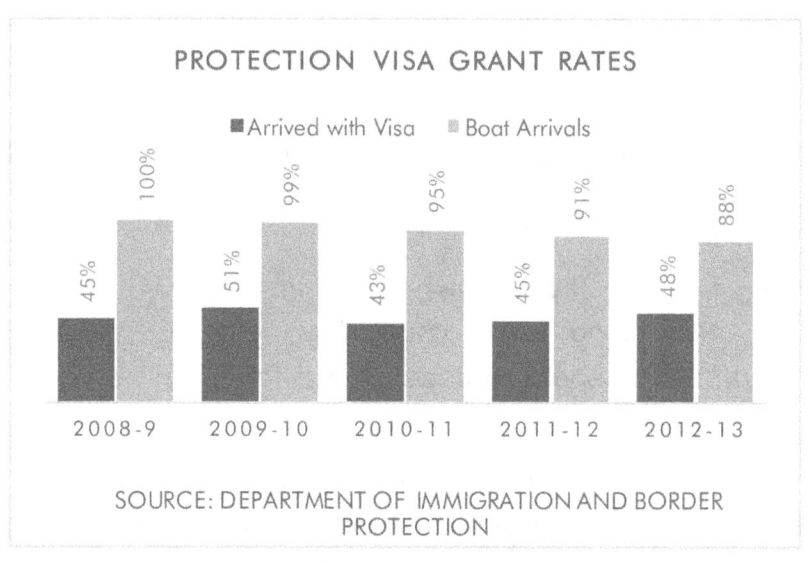

The argument that asylum seekers who arrive by boat take the spots of those who are "doing the right thing" waiting their turn in camps overseas operates on the fallacy that there is an orderly international system for resettling refugees in which a refugee registers and then waits for his or her turn. The reality is that less than 1% of the world's refugees are resettled each year, which renders any notion of an orderly queue meaningless. The UNHCR maintains a list of those in need of resettlement, and focuses on those with protection needs that cannot be met in the country of asylum. In 2015 the list identified 960,000 refugees in need of resettlement, yet only 81,893, yet only 8.5% were offered resettlement.[56] Moreover, those who are offered resettlement must meet the particular criteria of the country electing to resettle them. Canada, for example, does not include

48

unaccompanied children into its resettlement program.[57] Australia, which has the third largest resettlement program after the USA and Canada, does not accept any refugees from Indonesia. It set a resettlement target for 2015-16 of 11,000 places, which were divided between 6,000 places for refugees recommended for resettlement by the UNHCR and 5,000 places offered under Australia's "Special Humanitarian Program". This is defined by the government as follows:

> The Special Humanitarian Programme (SHP) is for people outside their home country who are subject to substantial discrimination amounting to gross violation of human rights in their home country. A proposer, who is an Australian citizen, permanent resident or eligible New Zealand citizen, or an organization that is based in Australia, must support applications for entry under the SHP.[58]

Given the necessity of sponsorship by an Australian resident this excludes refugees without connections in Australia from resettlement under the SHP.

Far from an orderly, predictable queue, resettlement functions more like a cruel lottery in which those who win receive a chance at building a new life, while the vast majority are not selected and are left to languish in impossible circumstances.

Finally, we should address the notion that asylum seekers arriving by boat are "illegals". This is the language of the Department of Immigration and Border

Protection, and is extremely misleading. Its effect is to demonise asylum seekers suggesting that they have done something wrong, perhaps even criminal, by seeking entry to Australia. They have not. Those arriving without visas are entering the country unlawfully, that is, without having been authorised to do so. They are however granted the right to do this by the Refugee Convention to which Australia is a signatory.

The Dangerous Refugee Myth

A third myth suggests that those who come by boat are likely to be criminals or terrorists. Australia does not keep statistics on crime rates by ethnicity nor by refugee status. We do keep statistics on imprisonment rates by country of birth, which show that people born in some countries, such as China, Fiji, and India have lower rates of imprisonment than those born in Australia, and that people born in other countries such as Lebanon and Sudan have higher rates of imprisonment.[59] These however provide little help in understanding refugee communities. To begin with, they provide data on migrant rather than refugee specific outcomes. Then they should be qualified by the fact that crime rates are higher amongst younger elements of any population, and given the age profile of migrant communities is younger than that of the broader Australian community, we would expect there to be higher rates of imprisonment amongst migrant communities. Moreover, crime rates are arguably much more connected with disadvantage and isolation, which are particularly high among some migrant communities. There is simply no evidence that crime rates among refugee communities are any higher than in the wider Australian population.

Regarding terrorist offences, Australia has had mercifully few terror attacks. Of those which have occurred on Australian soil the majority have been carried out by Australian citizens, with the greatest number of terrorist convictions belonging to white supremacist groups. Of the 800,000 refugees who have made their home in Australia since the end of the Second World War, four have been connected to terrorist related offences. At least one of these arrived in Australia when he was a young child and was radicalised while in Australia. Whether any of the four arrived by boat is unknown[60].

The Muslim Takeover Myth

This myth argues that waves of Muslims are entering the country as refugees, threatening either to turn us into a Muslim country, or creating a minority whose values are incompatible with the Australian way of life.

The reality is that unless there is a radical change to our immigration program, people who identify either culturally or religiously as Muslims will not in the foreseeable future constitute a large portion of the Australian population. A 2014 poll showed Australians, on average, estimate Muslims make up 18% of the Australian population.[61] The reality? According to the 2011 Census the proportion of the population identifying as Muslim was 2.2%. A recent Pew Forum demographic analysis has the Muslim population growing to 4.9% by 2050.[62]

And what of the claim that Muslims will not integrate? This of course begs the question, what does it mean to be Australian and what are "Australian values"? I take it that by this we mean commitment to the values of liberal democracy such as respect for the rule of law, freedom of religion, freedom of speech, freedom of thought, and to be committed to the well-being of one's fellow Australians. Within that framework there is room for great cultural and religious diversity.

A 2009 Monash university study found that more than 90% of Muslims agreed with the statement 'I can be a good Muslim and a good Australian.'[63] Surveys of Sydney Muslims conducted from 2011-2013 found that 84% of those interviewed felt they were Australian and that 90% said that it was important to them that their children be accepted as Australian.[64] Indeed, the Resilience and Ordinariness report concluded:

> Most research on Muslims living in Western countries has sampled at the deeper end of disaffection, reproducing discourses of non-integration. There is no compelling empirical evidence in Australia to support the case for widespread vulnerability to violent extremism among Muslims, nor is there any evidence to suggest widespread alienation. In fact, the results from this study into the ordinariness of the lives of Australian Muslims

show the contrary. The findings suggest a very strong sense of belonging amongst the Australian Muslim community. Australian Muslims have ordinary desires and needs, ranking education and employment as the highest of their concerns. They feel comfortable identifying as both Australian and Muslim. A substantial component of the sample had high levels of religiosity (particularly the face to face sample). However, religiosity was not associated with non-belonging, the data suggest the opposite. There were statistically significant positive associations between religiosity and belonging.[65]

Resettlement

Australia may not welcome asylum seekers who arrive on our shores undocumented, but each year it does provide 13,750 places to refugees and other people in humanitarian need, an at the time of writing this book it was government policy to increase that number to 18,750 in 2018-19. This includes asylum seekers who arrived in Australia on a valid visa, such as a study visa, and subsequently applied for protection; people in special humanitarian need but who don't strictly qualify as refugees; and refugees resettled from overseas. The latter group usually accounts for around half to two thirds of the available spaces in the humanitarian program. Each year approximately 30 countries provide resettlement services, and Australia consistently has the third-largest program in absolute terms (only the United States and Canada resettle more) and the largest on per capita basis.

Refugees who resettle in Australia are provided with caseworker support for the first 6-12 months to help them find their way into Australian life, are offered the opportunity to undertake English language classes, and are eligible for the same range of benefits as other members of the Australian community. They do not receive any other material benefits.[66]

Australians can be justifiably proud of this, but it needs to be remembered that the third largest resettlement program does not indicate Australia assumes a large part of the overall responsibility to protect. This is because resettlement provides a solution for less than 1% of the world's refugees each year. In 2015 2.34 million people were recognised as refugees by nations across the world, of which only 2,377 or 0.1%, were given refugee status in Australia. Considered over a longer period, the figures improve, but only marginally. Between 2006 and 2015 14,129,523 refugees were recognised, registered or resettled by the nations of the world. Australia recognised, registered or resettled 139,398, or 0.99%, of these. Per capita Australia is one of the wealthiest nations on earth, and from an absolute perspective has the thirteenth largest economy[67] yet it offers protection to less than 1% of the world's refugees.

The UNHCR uses three measures to indicate country capacity to provide protection to refugees: GDP per capita; refugees per 1,000 inhabitants; and refugees to 1000 m² of land. Australia ranks 69th, 63rd, and 120th respectively on these measures.[68] It is reasonable to conclude that despite its excellent resettlement program, Australia's share of the international protection burden is very small.

A Reality Check

There is a vast gulf between reality and perception in Australian beliefs and values around refugees and asylum seekers. Australia has an excellent refugee resettlement program, yet assumes a very small fraction of the burden of care. The bulk of the world's refugees reside in poor countries and only a very small percentage seek to come to Australia. Nnetheless we have managed to create a narrative that Australia faces a crisis. Rather than talking about how Australia can offer protection to refugees and asylum seekers we focus on how we can be protected from them!

Chapter 4
A Biblical Perspective

"An angel of the Lord appeared to Joseph in a dream and said, 'Get up, take the child and his mother, and flee to Egypt, and remain there until I tell you; for Herod is about to search for the child, to destroy him.' Then Joseph got up, took the child and his mother by night, and went to Egypt, and remained there until the death of Herod."

Gospel of Matthew

The nation was ruled by a murderous tyrant who ruthlessly crushed all opposition. Drunk with power, he even assassinated three of his children whom he feared may try to usurp him. The message was clear: no-one was safe.

The tyrant maintained a network of informers, which meant a loose word could see a person disappeared. People in this country learned the art of silence, even as the tyrant taxed them into poverty to fund a massive building program designed to project his greatness and massage his ego.

And now his fury was turned on a small town south of the capital. Rumours had been spreading that a child who was the true heir to the throne had been born there. The tyrant had always been neurotic about his legitimacy, and this new rumour fed his neurosis. Troops were dispatched. They arrived unannounced and a nightmare followed. Moving house to house, they seized all infant boys and stabbed them to death. For a few long hours the town was filled with the screams of parents and children, blood flowed in the streets, and the stench of death filled the air.

The child rumoured to be king escaped. Days before the soldiers arrived his father had a premonition that his son's life was endangered. He packed up the family and fled. When the news of the slaughter in his hometown reached him he was engulfed with sorrow and anger...and a determination to see his son to safety. And the only safe place was to be out of the country.

And so Joseph, Mary and their infant son, Jesus, passed from Israel to Egypt. Undocumented, unauthorised, irregular migrants. Refugees.

As we consider a biblically shaped response to the global refugee crisis, it is timely to remember that Jesus was a refugee.

The Responsibility of Power

The Genesis creation narratives picture humankind spreading across the earth building communities in which God is imaged. This means building communities that reflect the character of God - good, generous, gracious, loving, compassionate, just - and the purposes of God – societies where human beings flourish. This forms the foundation for the Bible's approach to power. Whenever it is held, power is to be used to serve these ends.

Governments are therefore responsible to secure justice for all under their care, even their most powerless citizens. Proverbs 31, for example, instructs kings that their prime responsibility is to secure the rights of the poor.

> The words of King Lemuel. An oracle that his mother taught him:
>
> No, my son! No, son of my womb!
> No, son of my vows!
> Do not give your strength to women,

> your ways to those who destroy kings.
> It is not for kings, O Lemuel,
> it is not for kings to drink wine,
> or for rulers to desire strong drink;
> or else they will drink and forget what has been decreed,
> and will pervert the rights of all the afflicted.
> Give strong drink to one who is perishing,
> and wine to those in bitter distress;
> let them drink and forget their poverty,
> and remember their misery no more.
> Speak out for those who cannot speak,
> for the rights of all the destitute.
> Speak out, judge righteously,
> defend the rights of the poor and needy.
>
> Proverbs 31:1-9

The "rights of the poor" are those things to which the poor are entitled, that they need in order to flourish, such as access to food (Genesis 1:29-30), rest (Exodus 20:8-9), and freedom from violence, exploitation and corruption (Exodus 3:7-10). In the Law of Israel these rights were given concrete expression in laws around social inclusion, debt and land (e.g. Deuteronomy 15; Leviticus 25).

The expectation that governments were responsible to secure justice for the vulnerable was not limited to Israel. Non-Israelite communities were called to the same standard. Sodom was destroyed because "she and her daughters had pride, excess of food, and prosperous ease, but did not aid the poor and needy." (Ezekiel

16:49); Amos 1-2 declares God's judgement on Damascus, Gaza, Tyre, Edom, Ammon, and Moab for gross violence against vulnerable communities; and Jonah is sent to Nineveh because of its outrages.

All too often however, rather than serving the interests of the vulnerable, power in biblical accounts was employed illegitimately. When the Israelites first asked for a human king, they were warned that even the best of kings would exploit their labour and take their land (1 Samuel 8:10-18). As the biblical story unfolds we see this warning realised within Israel and the nations. The book of Exodus describes the Egyptians enslaving the Israelites; Kings and Chronicles reveal King Solomon enslaving populations from the nations around Israel and taxing Israelites into poverty; the Gospels are written in the shadow of one of history's most ruthless and violent Empires; and the Revelation of John depicts this Empire as a monstrous beast devouring its enemies.

In such a world the presence of refugees is inevitable. Unsafe, persecuted, and denied the opportunity to thrive, people will flee regimes that threaten them. The Israelites fled Egypt for Canaan; David fled from a jealous Saul, finding refuge among the Philistines; Elijah fled from a furious Jezebel, for shelter in a cave on Mount Horeb; Joseph, Mary and Jesus fled a murderous Herod for safety in Egypt; the first Christians fled Jerusalem when a great persecution engulfed them; John wrote the Book of Revelation while exiled to Patmos island.

It should be no surprise that this pattern continues unabated in our time. Refugees are part of the fabric of a fallen world. The only question is how we will respond.

The Call to Anger and Compassion

One of the hallmarks of the biblical description of God is that God has compassion for the vulnerable, the exploited, the oppressed, and the poor and is angry at those who exploit, oppress, and neglect them. In one of the defining descriptions in the Old Testament, God is revealed to Moses on Mount Sinai as

> The Lord, the Lord,
> a God merciful and gracious,
> slow to anger,
> and abounding in steadfast love and faithfulness,
> keeping steadfast love for the thousandth generation,
> forgiving iniquity and transgression and sin,
> yet by no means clearing the guilty,
> but visiting the iniquity of the parents
> upon the children
> and the children's children,
> to the third and the fourth generation (Exodus 34:6-7)

This text describes both the compassion and the anger of God. We should remember that in the Old Testament iniquity expressed itself in an embrace of false gods and in the oppression of others. In a world where people do terrible things to one another, judgement is, at times, necessary to bring their oppressive ways to an end.

Evil cannot be met with a shrug of the shoulders, but must be resisted and defeated.

Yet the dominant note in God's dealings with people is compassion. God punishes where necessary, but the extent of his anger pales against the extent of his compassionate love. While his anger may last till the fourth generation, his mercy lasts to the thousandth.

The God of Scripture is not a hard God, throwing thunderbolts at the merest hint of dissent, but has a soft, patient and tender heart. This surprises many whose recollection of the God of the Old Testament is of a harsh God. Yet this fails to recognise the direction of God's compassion and anger. God's compassion is focused particularly upon the weak, vulnerable, exploited and oppressed and, more often than not, his anger is directed against those who marginalised, exploited and oppressed them.

Consider, for example, the prophet Isaiah who brings a thunderous declaration of judgement. Yet read a little closer and we discover it is not indiscriminate but directed against those who oppress and exploit in order to rescue those who suffer at their hands.

> Hear the word of the Lord, you rulers of Sodom! Listen to the teaching of our God, you people of Gomorrah!
>
> ... When you stretch out your hands, I will hide my eyes from you; even though you make many prayers, I will not listen; your hands are full of blood. Wash yourselves; make yourselves clean; remove the evil of your doings

from before my eyes; cease to do evil, learn to do good; seek justice, rescue the oppressed, defend the orphan, plead for the widow...

How the faithful city has become a whore! She that was full of justice, righteousness lodged in her—but now murderers! Your silver has become dross, your wine is mixed with water. Your princes are rebels and companions of thieves. Everyone loves a bribe and runs after gifts. They do not defend the orphan, and the widow's cause does not come before them.

Isaiah 1:10-23

The compassion of God for those who are vulnerable and weak and his anger at those who oppress them is seen supremely in the story of Jesus, who was marked by gentleness, mercy and a deep capacity to feel for others. Where Simon the Pharisee was disgusted by the woman who touched Jesus, Jesus was filled with compassion and goodwill for her (Luke 14:1-14). When a man with leprosy came to Jesus and begged to be made clean, Jesus was "filled with compassion" and healed him (Mark 1:40-45). When Jesus's friend Lazarus died, Jesus wept (John 11:17-44). And like God in the Old Testament, Jesus was angered by the hardheartedness of those who oppressed and marginalised the vulnerable. He "grew angry" when the Pharisees opposed his healing on the Sabbath and was "deeply distressed at their stubborn hearts" (Mark 3:1-6); in an age where wealth was commonly acquired by divesting the poor of their land

and livelihood, he pronounced woe upon the rich (Luke 6:24-25); and he condemned the religious leaders as hypocrites and blind guides (Matthew 23:1-35).

Scripture does not encourage us to dispassionately approach the vulnerable, exploited and oppressed. Rather, God calls us to be filled with compassion for those who suffer and godly, righteous anger at those who impose suffering upon them. We are to be engaged with our hearts as well as our minds. Compassion and righteous anger then should be at the forefront of our response to refugees, who are amongst the most vulnerable people in the world. Our call is to hear their stories and act out of a deep sense of empathy.

The Possibilities of Love

CNN television reporter Peter Arnett was once on assignment in the West Bank when a bomb exploded. Through a mass of wounded people strode a man carrying a little girl. She had been badly injured by the blast. The man begged Peter to take her to a hospital. As a member of the press he was one of the few able to get through the security cordon that police had thrown up. Peter agreed. He bundled the man and the girl into his car. The trip to the hospital was traumatic. Neither Peter nor the man knew if the little girl would survive.

They made it to the hospital, rushed the girl in, and waited anxiously while she was operated upon. After what seemed an eternity, the doctor came out with the tragic news that the little girl had died. The man collapsed in tears. Peter Arnett stumbled to comfort him as best he could. "I don't know what to say. I can't imagine what you must be going through. I've never lost a child."

The man turned and looked at Peter. "That girl was not my daughter. I'm an Israeli settler. She was a Palestinian. But there comes a time when each of us must realize that every child, regardless of that child's background, is a daughter or a son. There must come a time when we realize that we are all family."[83]

The words of that Israeli settler capture perfectly the biblical sentiment. The creation stories of Genesis remind us that we all bear the image and likeness of God, that this defines us, gives us value, and provides us with a common bond. We are not first and foremost Australian or Vietnamese or Afghani, but human. This means attachment to those who share our culture, ethnicity or nationality must always give way to the bonds of our common humanity.

This was a central concept in the Old Testament law.

> When a foreigner resides among you in your land, do not mistreat them. The foreigner residing among you must be treated as your native-born. Love them as yourself, for you were foreigners in Egypt. (Leviticus 19:33-34)
>
> The Lord your God is God of gods and Lord of lords, the great God, mighty and awesome, who shows no partiality and accepts no bribes. He defends the cause of

> the fatherless and the widow, and loves the foreigner residing among you, giving them food and clothing. And you are to love those who are foreigners, for you yourselves were foreigners in Egypt. (Deuteronomy 10:17-19)

Israel was never to reduce their God to the status of a tribal deity. Theirs was the God of gods, who brought all things into being and loved all nations and all people. God may have chosen Israel for a particular purpose, but this was not to be interpreted to mean God favoured Israel to the exclusion of others.

The most famous example of this comes in the book of Jonah. Sent to Nineveh to announce God's judgement, Jonah is aware God will forgive the Ninevites should they repent, and when this occurs grows angry.

> But this was very displeasing to Jonah, and he became angry. He prayed to the Lord and said, "O Lord! Is not this what I said while I was still in my own country? That is why I fled to Tarshish at the beginning; for I knew that you are a gracious God and merciful, slow to anger, and abounding in steadfast love, and ready to relent from punishing. (Jonah 4:1-2)

God's response to Jonah closes the book:

> Should I not be concerned about Nineveh, that great city, in which there are more than a hundred and twenty thousand persons who do not know their right hand from their left, and also many animals? (Jonah 4:11)

Just as God extended his love to all people, so the Israelites were to extend theirs. Foreigners were to be welcomed and treated with care. Like widows and fatherless children, foreigners were less likely to own land, more likely to serve as labourers or artisans, and more prone to neglect and abuse. The Israelites were not to take advantage of this, but were to make provision for foreigners and to treat them justly. And if their common humanity wasn't enough to inspire them, their historical memory of Egypt should. When Joseph's family arrived in Egypt they were welcomed with open arms. This however turned to oppression and extreme hardship. Knowing what it was to be welcomed and oppressed, Israel should embrace the former and reject the latter.

These themes are picked up by Jesus. We are to love even our enemies, for they are loved by God (Matthew 5:40-48). Moreover, given the explicit injunction of the Law to love the foreigner as oneself, his parable of the Good Samaritan (Luke 10:25-27) serves as a critique not only of purity obligations trumping the obligation to love those in need, but of national identity trumping the obligation to love foreigners in need. The context for the parable is a discussion between Jesus and a teacher of the Law who had identified love for God and love for neighbour as the two fundamental commands of the Law. But just who was his neighbour? Against those who limited the definition of neighbour to their fellow Israelite, the Samaritan shows that the neighbour is anyone in need.

The call to love beyond ethnic/national boundaries takes on new dimensions in the early church. In the visioning of the faith community, social and racial divides were overcome.

> Do not lie to each other, since you have taken off your old self with its practices and have put on the new self, which is being renewed in knowledge in the image of its Creator. Here there is no Gentile or Jew, circumcised or uncircumcised, barbarian, Scythian, slave or free, but Christ is all, and is in all. (Colossians 3:10-11)

In this vision Christ is the great equaliser. He brought the understanding that they were all created in God's image. Moreover, the logic of the gospel demanded that if he loved all and died for all, how could his followers do anything less? If people of all ethnicities and social status were welcomed by him and united to him, how could Christians maintain ethnic hatreds or distinctions based on social status? In place of hostility towards others, believers were encouraged to practice hospitality, to welcome strangers into their homes and feasts, to overcome evil with good, and to do good to all. In a world in which mercy was seen as a vice, Christians made it a cardinal virtue.

Critically, love for others is not simply a personal ethic, nor an ethic only for those with faith. It is a human ethic that should be the guiding value for both individuals and governments. Humankind was created to image God, and Scripture shows this is to govern both personal and community spheres. This is why love could be written into the laws of Israel; why humankind will one day be judged by the quality of our love; and why not only individuals, but nations are held to account for unloving behaviour. From this we may conclude that anything that prevents us from extending love to those in need diminishes us and robs those in need.

The Demands of Justice

We should not however think of our response to refugees in terms of charity. Rather, to offer love and protection to refugees is an act of justice.

Justice implies the existence of obligation and claim. States have an obligation to protect their citizens and citizens have a right to demand that their governments fulfil this obligation. Refugees, by definition, are people whose right to protection has been violated by their government.

But what of the obligations of the international community to those who have fled their homeland? In the worldview of many Australians how we respond is a matter of charity. That is, we have no obligation to provide asylum to any refugees, but do so as an act of kindness and generosity.

Given what we have said about the biblical call to love the foreigner and the person in distress, this argument fails. In the biblical worldview love is not an option but an obligation we owe to our neighbour. This is why in one breath the bible can call us to love the widow, the orphan, and the foreigner, and in the next describe action towards the widow, the orphan, and the foreigner in terms of justice.

> Do not deprive the foreigner or the fatherless of justice, or take the cloak of the widow as a pledge. Remember that you were slaves in Egypt and the LORD your God redeemed you from there. That is why I command you to do this. (Deuteronomy 24:17)

To love foreigners and to act justly toward them were essentially two sides of the same coin. Love called for welcome of foreigners, inclusion in the life of the community, and provision for their need. They were to rest on the Sabbath. If landless, they were to share in the harvest and to receive support from the tithe of Israel. Yet such acts of love were no more and no less a recognition that, because God was the Creator of the earth and all humankind, this was how every person deserved to be treated, and, because these acts of love were commanded in the Law, they were an obligation owed.

The rights of human beings to share in the abundance of the earth, to be safe, to be welcomed, to be able to live peacefully within community, do not evaporate when they cross a border. They are not civil rights but human rights. To meet them is our human obligation.

The Pattern of Redemption

The biblical narrative is a story of a redeeming God, who steps in to rescue people from situations of oppression and evil. So we see God rescuing the Israelites from slavery in Egypt.

> Then the Lord said, "I have observed the misery of my people who are in Egypt; I have heard their cry on account of their taskmasters. Indeed, I know their sufferings, and I have come down to deliver them from the Egyptians, and to bring them up out of that land to a good and broad land, a land flowing with milk and honey. (Exodus 3:7-8)

Once in the land, God's redemptive work continues. In the book of Judges, for example, we see God repeatedly delivering Israel from the hands of its enemies. We also witness God rescuing individuals from the oppressive hands of fellow Israelites.

> Father of orphans and protector of widows
> is God in his holy habitation.
> God gives the desolate a home to live in;
> he leads out the prisoners to prosperity,
> but the rebellious live in a parched land. (Psalm 68:5-6)

In the Gospels, Jesus liberates the demon possessed, heals the diseased and disabled, rescues a woman cowering before an angry mob ready to stone her, and offers forgiveness to those excluded by the religious system of the Pharisees. And of course, this culminates in the great act of redemption brought about by Christ's death and resurrection.

Redemption then is the dynamic that drives God's action in the world, and frames the biblical discussion of love, grace and justice. Love is modelled for us as extending oneself for others, especially those who are vulnerable, exploited and oppressed; grace sees God acting for others not because they have merited it, but because they need it; and justice is ultimately not focussed on retribution, on people getting what they deserve, but is God acting to liberate the oppressed regardless of whether they deserve it.

This same dynamic should drive our living. If humankind is made in the image and likeness of God, then our orientation to the world ought to be one of extending ourselves for the liberation and wellbeing of others.

> Let love be genuine; hate what is evil, hold fast to what is good; love one another with mutual affection; outdo one another in showing honour. Do not lag in zeal, be ardent in spirit, serve the Lord. Rejoice in hope, be patient in suffering, persevere in prayer. Contribute to the needs of the saints; extend hospitality to strangers.
>
> Bless those who persecute you; bless and do not curse them. Rejoice with those who rejoice, weep with those who weep. Live in harmony with one another; do not be haughty, but associate with the lowly; do not claim to be wiser than you are. Do not repay anyone evil for evil,

but take thought for what is noble in the sight of all. If it is possible, so far as it depends on you, live peaceably with all. Beloved, never avenge yourselves, but leave room for the wrath of God; for it is written, "Vengeance is mine, I will repay, says the Lord." No, "if your enemies are hungry, feed them; if they are thirsty, give them something to drink; for by doing this you will heap burning coals on their heads." Do not be overcome by evil, but overcome evil with good. (Romans 12:9-21)

Some Conclusions

These grand biblical themes expose Australian attitudes and public policy on refugees as sadly deficient, even godless. Our narrative is framed around protection of our borders, punishment of boat arrivals, and a refusal to equitably share the burden of the global refugee crisis. In stark contrast the biblical narrative calls us to recognise the asylum seeker and refugee as our neighbour, to offer hospitality and welcome, to do all we can to love the vulnerable foreigner.

Chapter 5
A Better Way

'"You shall love the Lord your God with all your heart, and with all your soul, and with all your mind." This is the greatest and first commandment. And a second is like it: "You shall love your neighbour as yourself." On these two commandments hang all the law and the prophets.'

Jesus

In my early 20s I was a delegate to a conference for young leaders sponsored by the Queen Elizabeth Silver Jubilee Trust. Delegates were selected from the business world, the media, politics, and community service organisations. For a week, we reflected on Australia's future. On the second day of the conference a University Professor made the case for a very small immigration program, arguing that it was necessary to preserve Australia's natural environment and economic wellbeing. During the Q and A session that followed I suggested that as a prosperous member of the international community we had an obligation to welcome and settle refugees. The Professor's response was that it was terrible that people were suffering but that we needed to do what was best for Australia. The discussion that followed suggested most delegates found the Professor convincing.

Two days later a woman who had made her way to Australia as a refugee stood at the lectern. She described the difficulty of life in Vietnam; her perilous flight to freedom on board a leaky boat; her arrival in Australia and the difficulty of starting a new life in a foreign culture; her determination to give back to the country that had given her a second chance; and her tireless effort to establish businesses that were now quite successful. The change in the delegates was incredible. Two days earlier they were ready to make Australia off-limits to people like the woman they had just heard. Hearing her story changed everything. She had ceased to represent a threat and instead was a person for whom we all felt deep empathy and admiration.

Delegates switched from thinking about how to protect Australia from the world, and focussed instead on how Australia could be a good global citizen. That is the focus of this chapter. What needs to change if we are to love our global neighbours?

Reframe the Discussion

The first thing we need to do is reframe the discussion around refugees, and particularly around asylum seekers. Research suggests that Australians have a generally high regard for refugees resettled from overseas, but a very low regard for asylum seekers who arrive by boat. There are widely held perceptions that asylum seekers represent a threat to our economic well-being and our social cohesion. Asylum seekers have been portrayed as undesirable, lacking in moral values, queue jumpers, terrorists, and certainly not legitimate refugees. A 2010 study, for example, found that almost 60% of those surveyed believed that asylum seekers came to Australia "for a better life" and only 24% thought that they were fleeing persecution.[84] This feeds concern that asylum seekers exploit Australia's democratic systems and processes through "queue jumping", that they will not integrate into Australian culture and so represent a threat to Australian values, and that they could be violent in their behaviour.

Media shock jocks and politicians have led the way in shaping this narrative. Yet as we have seen in previous chapters, it is clearly false.

We need a new discourse, one that empathises with both refugees overseas and asylum seekers arriving on our shores, that recognises our common humanity, and sees their protection as a high calling. We need to shift our focus from how we can protect ourselves from refugees to how we can protect those fleeing persecution, to see them as human beings who have made dangerous yet courageous bids for freedom, fleeing outrageous violence and persecution, in the process frequently traumatised by their experiences, and in need of our generous care. Rather than seeing refugees and asylum seekers as a threat to our social cohesion, we need to shape a discourse in which they are seen as enriching our society.

This does not mean we will naively neglect the need to control our borders, throw wide the gates to violent criminals, or ignore the challenges highly traumatised people can face in becoming part of the Australian community. Australia should continue to screen refugees for health and criminality risks and offer counselling and support to those who are traumatised. But we should not allow this to define our narrative. To do so cripples our humanity by turning the other into a danger to be avoided rather than a neighbour to be loved.

A marvellous example of this was an article by Hugh Riminton, published in the Daily Telegraph on January 6, 2017.[85] He opened by asking "What on earth are we going to do about those Sudanese kids in our suburbs?" The question feeds into anxiety about Sudanese refugees that is widespread in many parts of Australia. But rather than demonising Sudanese refugees and demanding tougher law enforcement, Riminton reframes the situation. He tells of John Mac, a Sudanese refugee he met in 2000, who became the first Sudanese refugee to gain a university degree in Australia, did postgraduate studies in Switzerland, yet could not get work in Australia outside of factory work. He eventually went back to west Africa where he started a school and was killed while seeking to protect his students. John's younger brother, Deng, who arrived in Australia a traumatised former child soldier and was illiterate, went on to study law and began his own practise. He has raised over $100,000 for charity and in 2016 was the NSW Australian of the Year.

Redefine the National Interest

Foreign policy is usually based on "securing the national interest", a concept that arose with the development of the modern nation state.[86] This is unlikely to change in the near future, but we should articulate the notion that the national interest is far broader than our material prosperity.

In a democracy, the national interest is simply the set of shared priorities regarding relations with the rest of the world. It is broader than strategic interests, though they are part of it. It can include values such as human rights and democracy, if the public feels that those values are so important to its identity that it is willing to pay a price to promote them.[87]

Should we not define our national interest as including our material prosperity, our social cohesiveness, our ecological sustainability, the construction of our national character, and a determination to be a good global citizen? Should we not aspire to be a good, even a great, nation and define greatness not merely in terms of our own accomplishments but also in terms of our contribution toward the creation of a just and peaceful world?

Seek A Global Solution

The refugee crisis is too large for any single nation to resolve on its own. As long as systemic violence and injustice exist, we will see flows of refugees. To meet this challenge, the nations of the world need to make the durable solutions of safe return, integration in the host state, or resettlement in a third country available to all refugees. This will require intensive short term efforts to find a solution for all those who are currently refugees and, in the longer term a system of durable solutions that are sufficient to the need.

Invest in Peace

The international community can invest in peace using soft power (influence by non-coercive means), payments (influence by creating economic incentives and assistance), and, arguably, hard power (influence by coercion).[88] While the international community will not be able to prevent all outbreaks of war, nor persecution of minorities, investments in peace can reduce the likelihood and length of conflict. For example, development economist Paul Collier explored the place of aid to conflicted states. He argued that slow economic growth and low income are key risks that lead to rebellions and coups. In pre-conflict states with poor governance, inflows of foreign aid do little to change the likelihood of conflict, for low capacity government is unable to produce the policies required to stimulate economic growth. In a post-conflict situation, however, even where there is poor governance, aid can make a big difference by funding the rebuilding of the nation, which will reduce the risk of a slide back into conflict and encourage the emergence of more stable government.[89]

Invest in Countries of Asylum

In chapter 2 we noted that the bulk of the world's refugee populations are hosted by a relatively small number of low and middle income countries; that this places a substantial burden on communities, governments and economies; yet that poorer host communities and the institutions created to assist them are chronically underfunded.

As long as human greed and violence exist it is inevitable that some countries will fall into conflict, that large swathes of their populations will flee to neighbouring countries, and that most will wait for peace so that they might return home. It is not however inevitable that those host countries and the UNHCR will be chronically underfunded and unable to provide services to their refugee populations. In 2015 the UNHCR budget shortfall was $3.574 billion. Australia contributed just over $46 million (USD) to the UNHCR.[90] The largest donor was the USA with $1.35 billion. These are substantial sums of money, but are very small relative to total government spending. The Australian Government spent $298 billion (USD) in 2015.[91] A fully funded UNHCR is a very achievable goal.

Resettle Greater Numbers

The tyranny of distance means Australia is unlikely to have large numbers of people arriving by sea or air and claiming asylum. Australia's main contribution will therefore be as a country of resettlement and as a provider of support to countries of asylum.

At the very least, the international community should ensure that all those needing resettlement are offered it without having to wait years and even decades. Responsibility for this arguably belongs with those nations of middle and higher income that are politically stable, have relatively few asylum claims, and have the capacity to resettle substantial numbers. Australia, consistently ranked by the Credit Suisse annual wealth reports as one of the top three wealthiest nations on a per capita basis, and consistently ranked as one of the three most highly developed nations by the United Nations Human Development Index, is well-placed to play a more substantial role. Australia already has the third largest resettlement program, after the United States and Canada, but our share of the overall global protection burden is very low. At the end of 2014, for example, Australia was the 69th ranked nation in terms of refugees to income per capita and the 67th ranked nation in terms of refugees per 1000 inhabitants.

How many refugees should Australia resettle? There is no simple answer, but if we assume that one-third of the world's refugees would choose resettlement if the opportunity were available and that the responsibility to resettle was shared equitably among the world's high income nations, Australia, with 2.8% of high-income GDP[92] would be responsible for resettling around 180,000 of the world's existing population of refugees and asylum seekers. This would not necessarily occur in a single year, but could be spread out over a number of years.

The existing refugee population has built up over many years. If the world came together and found durable solutions for all existing refugees, what would be required going forward? The answer depends on the number of people who become refugees in any given year. The table below shows the number of people who became refugees or asylum seekers in the years 2011-2015 and Australia's resettlement fair share for those years.

YEAR	NO. NEW REFUGEES	AUSTRALIA'S FAIR SHARE
2011	800,000	7,457
2012	1,100,000	10,253
2013	2,500,000	23,302
2014	2,900,000	27,031
2015	3,800,000	35,419

A consensus is emerging around the notion that Australia should increase its humanitarian migration program from the current 13,750 places per annum and projected 18,750 by 2018-19 to 30,000 places per annum. The target of 30,000 is suggested by the Refugee Council of Australia.[93] A similar suggestion was made by the Expert Panel on Asylum Seekers appointed by the government in 2012, which recommended an increase to 27,000 places per annum.

Two questions are commonly posed to proposals like this. First, some ask whether Australia can absorb numbers at this level without damaging the social fabric of our communities. The answer is that yes we can. Australia has one of the most culturally diverse populations in the world, with 28% of those living in Australia born overseas. At September 30, 2016 Australia's population was 24,405,442 people, which means over 6.8 million were born overseas. We have an annual migration program of around 190,000 permanent migrants and over 600,000 temporary migrants such as student and people on working holidays per year. Yet we enjoy tremendous social cohesion. Contrary to popular perceptions, at the same time the proportion of Australian's born overseas has been going up, the incidence of violent crime has been declining (the one sad exception to this appears to be an increasing incidence of domestic violence).

CRIME	VICTIMISATION RATE	
	2010	2015
Homicide	2.1	1.8
Physical Assault	2.9	2.1
Sexual Assault	0.3	0.3
Break in	3.0	2.7

SOURCE: ABS 4510.0

What then of the financial cost of increasing the refugee intake? Can Australia afford it? Research consistently shows that while there is a short-term cost, in the longer term, refugees are a net benefit to our economy and contribute positively to our social capital.[94]

Nonetheless, there is a short-term cost, which is approximately $56,000 per refugee per year.[97] Increasing our humanitarian intake from the projected 18,750 in 2018-19 to 30,000 would therefore add around $630 million per annum to the budget. While this is a substantial amount it should be remembered that in

2013-14 Australia spent almost $1.4 billion detaining just a few thousand refugees on Manus Island and Nauru and over $1 billion a year in the following two years.[98] As these years included large upfront investments in infrastructure, the costs of offshore detention have declined, but closing the offshore facilities would still yield a saving of $2 billion over the four years to 2020[99] that would compensate for 80% of the cost of increasing our refugee resettlement program to 30,000.

Develop a Regional Protection System

In 2015 the Asia-Pacific was home to 3.5 million refugees, 1.9 million internally displaced people and 1.4 million stateless people.[100] Yet it is not a region that is welcoming of them. Many nations in our region, including Indonesia, Malaysia, Singapore, Laos, Vietnam, Thailand, and Bangladesh, are not signatories to the Refugee convention. In the absence of both a shared commitment to Convention principles and a cooperative approach, each nation does what it can to disincentivise the arrival of refugees for fear that if they don't they may well attract even more refugees. We have already traced, for example, the evolution of Australia's deterrence policies and noted the harsh treatment of refugees in Malaysia.

The only way to turn this around is to forge a regional approach that sees countries sharing responsibility for providing protection. If, for example, it was agreed that the middle and higher income nations of the region would share responsibility for making durable solutions available to refugees, the "need" to deter would evaporate. Jointly funded and operated processing facilities could be established in countries that are common places of first asylum or transit, such as Malaysia and Indonesia. Knowing they would not be left with all refugees who entered their borders, these countries could commit to fair and decent treatment of asylum seekers, the centres would process refugee claims quickly, and all found to be refugees would be offered a place of asylum or resettlement in a middle or higher income country in the region.

To many people this may sound hopelessly naïve. There is, however, historical precedent in the internationally cooperative approach adopted in the wake of the Vietnamese refugee crisis that followed the Vietnam War. W. Courtland Robinson described the situation that led to the cooperative approach:

> In the summer of 1979, more than 350,000 Vietnamese and Laotian refugees were scattered in camps from Thailand to Hong Kong, and another half a million Cambodians were massed at the Thai border. Local promises of temporary asylum collapsed. Vietnamese boats were pushed back by the hundreds, and thousands of Cambodians were forced back at gunpoint into their country. Sea pirates raided helpless refugee boats, raping and plundering at will. Camps were filled to bursting and still they came, with untold numbers perishing along the way.[101]

A UN conference attended by 65 governments sought to resolve the crisis, with three critical outcomes. First, the government of Vietnam promised to make it possible for those wanting to flee the country to leave in an orderly fashion, direct to countries of resettlement. Second, the international community increased its resettlement pledges from 125,000 places to 260,000 places. Third, Indonesia and the Philippines agreed to establish regional processing centres. Although it was not formally agreed, it was understood that these countries would welcome refugees on the assumption that they would be permanently resettled somewhere else.

As countries followed through on their commitments the flow of illegal departures from Vietnam fell dramatically and over 450,000 refugees were resettled from the south-east Asian refugee camps. Resurgent numbers of Vietnamese boat arrivals in 1987 and 1988 led to a collapse of the consensus, and the forging of a new agreement, the Comprehensive Plan of Action, in 1989. It had five objectives:

1. to create a pathway by which people could leave Vietnam in an orderly fashion;
2. to provide first asylum to all asylum seekers until their status had been determined;
3. to determine the refugee status of asylum seekers in accordance with international standards;
4. to resettle those found to be refugees in third countries;

5. to return those not found to be refugees to their home countries and ensure they were reintegrated there.

The agreement was imperfectly implemented, but nonetheless achieved substantial outcomes. Countries of first asylum such as Indonesia did accept more asylum seekers; from 1990-1995 over half a million refugees were resettled in third countries; and those found not to be refugees were repatriated, often against their will, to their home country. This last measure was extremely controversial, particularly as not all participants expressed confidence in the processing of asylum claims. Nonetheless, the CPA, for all its flaws in implementation, yielded some extremely positive outcomes and showed that a regionally cooperative approach that involved countries of origin, countries of first asylum, and countries of resettlement could work.

While it would be ideal to develop a widely multilateral approach, as occurred with the CPA, Australia could begin on a bilateral basis. This was a recommendation of the Expert Panel on Asylum Seekers in 2012, which suggested that Australia should open negotiations with Indonesia and Malaysia.

Resolve the Situation of Those in Offshore Detention, On Bridging Visas and on TPVs

Movement toward a regional approach would provide the framework for Australia to abandon its deterrence focussed approach in favour of a protection focussed approach. In the meantime, two of the more shameful dimensions of the deterrence approach – offshore indefinite detention and the issuing of temporary protection visas, could be immediately resolved.

The politics of asylum are such that it is difficult to imagine either the Coalition or the ALP implementing policies that resulted in a resumption of boat arrivals to Australia. Mandatory offshore detention, the issuing of temporary protection visas to boat arrivals already in Australia, and the interception and turning back of boats were introduced as part of increasingly severe measures to deter asylum seekers from making their way to Australia by boat. Arguably, the introduction of boat turnbacks has made offshore detention and TPVs redundant. That is, the ability of the Australian Navy to intercept and return boats is all that is necessary to deter most asylum seekers from setting out for Australia and to prevent the arrival in Australia of those that do seek to make the journey. This makes it feasible for the Australian Government to immediately offer resettlement to those currently detained on Manus Island and Nauru (or to find resettlement options for them in countries with sufficient prosperity and rule of law to ensure they could enjoy protection and the opportunity to rebuild their lives). Likewise, the practise of offering temporary protection visas could be abandoned. The Government could offer permanent protection visas to all those on TPVs and the 35,000 asylum seekers (as at September 2016)[102] who arrived by boat in previous years and are still waiting for their claim to refugee status to be assessed.

Some Conclusions

The second verse of Advance Australia Fair includes these words: "For those who've come across the seas, we've boundless plains to share." It is time we made good on this declaration. Our current policies fail the tests of love, justice and redemption. We can however adopt better policies, such as those outlined in this chapter.

Chapter 6
Where To From Here?

There are those who look at things the way they are, and ask why... I dream of things that never were, and ask why not?

Robert Kennedy
Former US Attorney General

In 1784 the Vice Chancellor of Cambridge University made the morality of slavery the theme of the University's annual essay competition. He announced this theme after learning that a slave ship captain had thrown 133 of the slaves he was transporting into the sea.

Thomas Clarkson, a student with no prior interest in slavery but a strong desire to obtain literary glory, won the essay competition. Writing the essay changed him. As he left university for his first appointment as a deacon in the Anglican Church, he found that slavery

> wholly engrossed my thoughts.... Coming in sight of Wades Mill in Hertfordshire, I sat down disconsolate on the turf by the roadside and held my horse. Here a thought came into my mind, that if the contents of the Essay were true, it was time some person should see these calamities to their end.[113]

Clarkson knew he had to be that person, so he abandoned a career in the Church for a lifetime of activism against slavery.

At the close of the eighteenth century, the slave trade was a large, thriving business. Prominent families used slaves and held interests in the slave business, a vast swathe of people depended on slavery for their livelihoods, and public opinion was undisturbed by it. When Clarkson threw in his lot with a small group of Quakers in opposition to the trade, the odds of success seemed impossible.

On May 22, 1787, Clarkson and about a dozen others met in the James Phillip Bookstore for the first official meeting of the Committee of the Slave Trade. They devised a strategy to gather intelligence on the trade, expose its inhumanity via pamphlets, posters, and public lectures, and build momentum to ban the British slave trade. Clarkson became their only full-time, antislavery campaigner. He travelled tirelessly throughout England, seeking to gather intelligence on the slave trade and to draw people's attention to its cruelty and inhumanity.

The task was incredibly difficult. Few of those involved in the slavery business would talk to him, he received death threats and at least one attempt on his life, many mocked him. In that first year he noted:

> I began now to tremble, for the first time, at the arduous task I had undertaken, of attempting to subvert one of the branches of the commerce of the great place which was then before me.... I questioned whether I should even get out of it alive.

Yet the tide of opinion began to turn. Petitions containing thousands of names found their way to Parliament. More people joined the cause, including the potter Josiah Wedgewood, whose relief of a kneeling slave with the words "Am I not a man and a brother?" became a popular and influential adornment, and parliamentarian William Wilberforce, who championed the cause in Parliament. Hundreds of thousands stopped using slave-harvested sugar, the major slave-produced good in England, and instead used slave-free sugar. The autobiography of freed slave Olauda Equiano became a best seller, and many heard him speak.

Within five years of that first meeting at the James Phillip Bookstore, public opinion had turned against the slave trade. Parliament, however, would take longer to conquer. William Wilberforce became the spearhead of the parliamentary campaign. Like Clarkson, Wilberforce came up against fierce opposition and derision. Admiral Horatio Nelson, for example, condemned "the damnable doctrine of Wilberforce and his hypocritical allies." Yet Wilberforce also found the support of colleagues such as the Prime Minister, William Pitt.

Bills against the trade were introduced in 1791, 1792, 1793, 1797, 1798, 1799, 1804, and 1805, all without success, until on February 27, 1807, a bill for the abolition of the slave trade passed the House by a vote of 283 to 16.

Who would have thought that a Latin essay would unleash a movement by which the slave trade would be brought to its knees? Who would have guessed that the movement would bring together Vice Chancellors, Quakers, pottery makers, ordinary citizens, freed slaves, activists, and politicians, each playing their part for such a tremendous outcome?

I recount this story to make a simple point: public opinion and policy can change. In fact, it changes quite regularly. When I was a child, smoking was an acceptable practice. People smoked in their workplaces, their homes, and in public. I was seven when my father, a lawyer, gave up smoking, becoming one of the few people in his company who abstained. My children are growing up in a society where it is both illegal and frowned upon to smoke in workplaces, restaurants, train stations, and most other public spaces. Or consider sexual morality. In my lifetime laws against adultery, divorce and homosexuality have all changed dramatically, along with popular attitudes.

There is no reason public policy and attitudes toward asylum seekers and refugees can't shift just as dramatically. Indeed, the story of the ending of the transatlantic slave trade reminds us that change is possible if it is tackled simultaneously on two levels, the political and the public.

One of the most significant actions of the antislavery movement was to raise the awareness of the public about the horror of the slave trade. Most people were simply unaware. Research into the widespread negative attitude towards asylum seekers amongst Australians suggests that it is based on a perception that asylum seekers represent a threat to our economic well-being and our social cohesion. As noted earlier, asylum seekers have been portrayed as undesirable, lacking in moral values, queue jumpers, potentially terrorists, and certainly not legitimate refugees.

These fears are based on misunderstandings and false beliefs. Given the positive attitude that exists toward refugees who are assessed overseas, there are good grounds for believing that Australian attitudes can change and will change as people hear the stories of asylum seekers, as their fears are addressed, and as they let go of false beliefs.

Secondly, we need action at a political level. Politicians should stop demonising asylum seekers and instead craft a new rhetoric that portrays them as courageous people fleeing persecution. New policies are also required that focus on protection.

There are seven things you can do to help effect these changes.

First, decide that you will not remain neutral. Like Thomas Clarkson, recognise that "if the contents of the Essay were true, it was time some person should see these calamities to their end."

Second, stay informed on the issue and share your insights with family and friends. Reading this book provides a good orientation. The Refugee Council of Australia (refugeecouncil.org.au), Asylum Seeker Resource Centre (asrc.org.au), and Amnesty International (amnesty.org.au) have excellent resources.

Third, tell stories. They are much better than facts for changing people's hearts and minds. Stories allow us to empathise, to stop demonising people based on the group they belong to and to see them as unique individuals. Read the stories in this book, watch stories online (UNHCR has a great refugee stories channel), and read refugee autobiographies. Share what you find on your social media, by telling stories around the dinner table, by loaning a friend the book you read. Immerse yourself in refugee stories and share them with your family, friends and work colleagues.

Fourth, participate in refugee advocacy campaigns. Advocacy is the act of influencing decision makers to make just decisions and it is something many Christians have not strongly engaged with. Yet it has proven very successful when three things come together:

a) a champion within the political system, such as William Wilberforce was in the English Parliament;

b) achievable policy proposals. Advocates are often passionate idealists who present politicians with asks that are morally laudable but politically difficult. Politicians both lead the public and are constrained by the public, so any arguments for change you bring need to be changes for which they can gain public support; and

c) substantial public support. Public support for change, demonstrated by letters, emails, videos and visits to MPs communicate to politicians that there is support for change within the community.

A good advocacy campaign will see community groups working together to build public support, will develop politically achievable asks, and will support champions in the Parliament. A Just Cause seeks to connect churches into good campaigns. You can find more detail at ajustcause.com.au.

Fifth, if you're a church leader consider running a preaching and bible study series on the issue. This book contains a bible study discussion guide (see the back pages) and preaching ideas can be downloaded from the refugee page at ajustcause.com.au

Sixth, get involved in serving refugees. For example, you might volunteer time or donate goods to a local organisation working with refugees. You could also support not-for-profits that run programs for refugees, such as Baptcare's Sanctuary program and Baptist World Aid Australia's humanitarian work with Syrian refugees in Lebanon and Burmese refugees in Malaysia.

Seventh, if you are a person of faith, pray.

Together, let us create an Australia that embodies a loving and just response to refugees and asylum seekers.

Bible Studies

The Bible studies included here will help small groups explore the issues around refugees and asylum seekers raised in this book. The studies aim to:

- build empathy for refugees and asylum seekers by exposing group members to their stories;
- build a response to the global refugee crisis that is based upon fact rather than popular mythology;
- explore biblical themes that impact upon our approach to refugees and asylum seekers;
- help group members identify practical ways they can respond.

Each study consists of four parts:

- opening up the issue: questions that allow participants to launch into the issue by reflecting on what they have read and where they currently stand;
- exploring the Bible: reading biblical texts that are relevant to the issue and exploring what they mean;
- applying it: asking how the biblical teaching applies practically to our response to refugees and asylum seekers;
- praying together: praying around the issues raised in the studies.

Groups should be able to complete each study in 60 to 75 minutes. Group leaders should ensure the video clips that begin each study are ready for viewing. You can connect a laptop to a smart TV or access the internet directly through a smart TV. Leaders should also have cards and markers available for each study.

Group leaders should be aware that the issue may prove controversial and discussion may get impassioned. It will be important to exercise listening skills and avoid judging.

Furthermore, group leaders should be aware that while we may agree on the biblical values that should drive our approach to refugees and asylum seekers, when it comes to the enacting of those values in policy there will always be room for disagreement. We should work hard to respect those disagreements.

Discussion Group Study 1

Before this study you should read chapter 1 of this book.

Introduction

The subject of refugees & asylum seekers raises strong emotions and opinions in the Australian population. Some Australians believe we should take far more refugees, others that we should take far fewer. Some people distinguish between "genuine refugees", whom they are happy to welcome to Australia, and those they suspect to be "economic refugees" or "unworthy refugees". Some people are concerned that refuges won't assimilate, that they might be violent, and even terrorists. In this first session we will listen to the stories of refugees to try to begin sorting our way through some of these questions.

Opening Up the Issue

1. On a set of cards write a list of the things you hear people say about refugees and asylum seekers, using a new card for each statement. Place the cards somewhere everyone can see them. What values and concerns do these reflect?

2. Watch the story of Scisa Rumenge (https://youtu.be/6vgVfqsHqhQ). His is one of the stories told in chapter 1. How does Scisa's story impact you? How might listening to the stories of refugees impact the way we respond to them?

Exploring the Bible

3. According to the Bible Jesus and his parents were refugees. Read Matthew 2:13-23. What parallels do you see between the story of Jesus and the stories you read in chapter 1 of this book? Does the fact that Jesus was a refugee impact the way you think about refugees?

4. The book of Exodus describes God's liberation of the Israelites from slavery in Egypt. Read Exodus 1:1-22 and 3:1-10. What does this teach you about how God responds to the oppression and persecution of human beings? What significance does this have for how we respond to refugees?

Applying it

5. The Convention Relating to the Status of Refugees defines a refugee as a person who

> "owing to a well-founded fear of being persecuted for reasons of race, religion, nationality, membership of a particular social group or political opinion, is outside the country of his nationality and is unable, or owing to such fear, is unwilling to avail himself of the protection of that country; or who, not having a nationality and being outside the country of his or her habitual residence, is unable, or, owing to such fear, is unwilling to return to it."

To be considered a refugee a person must be assessed as having met these criteria. The assessment is carried out by the governments of countries to which refugees flee or by the UN High Commission for Refugees. Those who have been assessed as meeting the criteria are described as "refugees", where those who have applied for a recognition but whose assessment is not yet complete are described as "asylum seekers". This means that anybody classed as a "refugee" has a story similar to the ones you read in chapter 1. How does this impact the way you think about and respond to refugees?

Praying Together

6. Think about the story from chapter 1 that impacted you the most. Write the name of the refugee from that story on a card, and place the card on top of the question/statement cards you compiled in question 1. We understandably have questions about refugees, but these must never stop us from responding to refugees as fellow human beings who have experienced great suffering and are in need of protection. Spend time praying together, asking God to help you resolve your questions during this Bible study series, and asking for God's protection for the refugees whose stories you have heard.

Discussion Group Study Two

Before this study you should read chapter 2 of this book.

Introduction

Across the world today more than 20 million people live as refugees, that is, they face persecution in their home country and have been forced to leave to find safety. In this study we will consider their situation and how the international community is responding to them.

Opening Up the Issue

1. Watch the "Syria's Lost Generation: The Plight of the Youngest Refugees" at https://youtu.be/4iaJPafQrqY How does this impact you? How does it impact the way you understand the situation of refugees?

2. Take 3 cards and write on them the three most important things you learned from reading Chapter 2 of this book. Place the cards somewhere everybody can see them and share your thoughts with the group.

Exploring the Bible

3. Read Deuteronomy 10:17-19. In the ancient near east widows, orphans and foreigners were the people most vulnerable to exploitation, marginalisation and poverty. In an age when the gods were commonly thought to stand on the side of the king and others with power, the Bible reveals God stands on the side of the vulnerable. Why do you think this is? How do you think God defended them? How might this apply to refugees today?

4. "The creation stories of Genesis remind us that we all bear the image and likeness of God, that this defines us, gives us value, and provides us with a common bond. We are not first and foremost Australian or Vietnamese or Afghani, but human. This means attachment to those who share our culture, ethnicity or nationality must always give way to the bonds of our common humanity". Do you agree? What implications does this have for the way we respond to refugees?

Applying it

5. Chapter 2 argues that the international community is failing to live up to the promises it has made to protect those who are fleeing persecution. Do you agree?
....

Why/why not? How does this shape the way you think about refugees and the global refugee crisis?

6. On the basis of what you learned in Chapter 2 and have discussed in this study, do you think that wealthier nations like Australia have a responsibility to do more? Why/why not? What might this look like?

Praying Together

7. Spend time praying for the international community and its response to refugees.

Discussion Group Study Three

Before this study you should read chapter 3 of this book.

Introduction

Australia's response to refugees has been marked by two distinct trends. First, we have a long history of resettling refugees from other countries. Second, we have closed ourselves off to asylum seekers arriving by boat, implementing extremely harsh measures to deter them from seeking out Australia as a place of safety. In this study we will explore this further.

Opening Up the Issue

1. Ahn Doh is a popular comedian who came to Australia as a refugee from Vietnam. Review his story (told in chapter 1) and/or view the interview with Ahn found at https://youtu.be/Z3vkLBy_P30. How does Ahn's story challenge popular ideas Australians hold about refugees?

2. Take 3 cards and write on them the three most important things you learned from reading Chapter 3 of this book. Place the cards somewhere everybody can see them and share your thoughts with the group.

3. Chapter 3 argues that Australia has turned its back on the principle that it should offer protection to asylum seekers and has created a series of myths to justify the action. Do you agree? Why/why not? Which of the myths have you heard before?

Exploring the Bible

4. Read Matthew 25:31-46. In the time of Jesus there was a live debate as to what it meant to live as the people of God. The Pharisees, for example, focused upon observing the Law right down to the last detail. According to this parable what is the hallmark of living as the people of God? What are the implications for our approach to asylum seekers who arrive on our shores?

Applying it

5. Brainstorm ways you and your group could serve refugees and asylum seekers in Australia. Choose one and implement it this week.

Praying Together

6. Spend time praying for people fleeing violence and seeking asylum in Australia, that they would find a

place of safety, healing and the opportunity for a fresh start. Pray also for our government, that it might enact policies that are just, merciful and loving.

Discussion Group Study Four

You should read Chapter 5 of this book before this study.

Introduction

In the first three studies we focussed on the situation of refugees and the failure of the international community to provide the protection they need. In this study we will focus on some solutions. What is it that countries like Australia, churches, and citizens can do to care for and serve refugees?

Opening Up the Issue

1. View Balan's story at https://vimeo.com/73546739 What issues does it raise for you?

2. Take 3 cards and write on them the three most important things you learned from reading Chapter 5 of this book. Place the cards somewhere everybody can see them and share your thoughts with the group.

Exploring the Bible

3. Read the parable of the Good Samaritan in Luke 10:25-37. What implications does the story have for how Australia should respond to refugees and asylum seekers?

Applying it

4. Chapter 5 argues that to resolve the international refugee crisis the international community needs to invest in durable solutions – in peace initiatives that allow refugees to safely return to their home country; in opportunities for refugees to integrate into the life of their host countries; and in increasing the number of resettlement opportunities. Do you agree? Why/why not? What should Australia's role be?

5. Chapter 5 argues that we need a regional framework for processing and settling refugees in the Asia Pacific. It pointed to the cooperative approach that followed the Vietnamese refugee crisis as an example of how this might be achieved. Do you think such can approach is viable? Why/why not?

6. Think back to Balan's story that you viewed at the start of this study. What might a church like yours do to care for someone like Balan?

Praying Together

7. Spend time praying for a new approach to the refugee crisis among our political leaders both in Australia and globally. Pray for Balan.

Action Week

For your final meeting in this small groups series, focus on what you can do as a group and as a church in response to what you have learned.

Group members should read Chapter 6 before coming to the group. Someone should volunteer to discover what refugee services exist within your community and what their needs are. Someone else should volunteer to find out what advocacy campaigns are running and ways that churches can be involved in them.

Spend this meeting developing an action plan for how you will engage with refugees and asylum seekers. You might like to begin with the suggestions at the end of Chapter 6.

ENDNOTES

[1] Araujo, D., "Persecution Continues: Political Reform in Myanmar May Not Be The Progress We Think It Is", Patheos blog, January 10, 2014, http://www.patheos.com/blogs/christandpopculture/2014/01/persecution-continues-political-reform-in-myanmar-may-not-be-the-progress-we-think-it-is/. Accessed June 2014

[2] Sollom, R., Beyrer, C., Richards, A., Johnson, R., Suwanvanichkij, V., Parmar, P., Mullany, L., Bradshaw, J. *Life under the Junta: Evidence of Crimes against Humanity in Burma's Chin State*, Physicians for Human Rights, 2011

[3] Seng, Theary *Daughter of the Killing Fields: Asrei's Story*, Fusion Press, 2005

[4] Ruchyahana, John, *The Bishop of Rwanda. Finding Forgiveness Among a Pile of Bones*. Thomas Nelson, 2007

[5] UNHCR, "New Year heralds fresh beginning for Rwandan refugees leaving Pakistan", Feb 2, 2013, http://www.unhcr.org/50e448ac9.html. Accessed April 2014

[6] Megan Camm, "Conflict In Congo", World Policy Journal (Winter 2011/2012)

[7] Alison Parker, *Hidden in Plain View: Refugees Living Without Protection in Nairobi and Kampala* (Human Rights Watch, November 2002)

[8] Scisa's story compiled from UNHCR refugee stories youtube channel https://www.youtube.com/watch?v=6vgVfqsHqhQ and Becky Palstom, "Profile of a musician in a refugee camp in Kenya", https://beta.prx.org/stories/59191

[9] Li, H, "Second Annual Address on Immigration and Citizenship", Museum of Democracy, June 16, 2011. Transcript available at http://www.multicultural.sa.gov.au/__data/assets/pdf_file/0018/5922/second-annual-address-hieu-van-le-2011.pdf.pdf

[10] UNHCR, *Global Trends 2015*

[11] UNHCR, *Global Trends 2015*

[14] UNHCR, *Global Trends 2015*

[15] UNHCR, *Global Trends 2015*

[16] Gomez and Christensen, "The Impacts of Refugees on Neighboring Countries: A Development Challenge" World Development Report

2011 Background Note (World Bank, July 29 2010); Shellito, K. (2016). "The Economic Effect of Refugee Crises on Host Countries and Implications for the Lebanese Case," Joseph Wharton Research Scholars.
[17] Shellito, K. (2016). "The Economic Effect of Refugee Crises"
[18] World Bank Lebanon page. http://www.worldbank.org/en/country/lebanon/overview#1. Accessed January 11,2017
[19] Shekhar Aiyar, Bergljot Barkbu, Nicoletta Batini, Helge Berger, Enrica Detragiache, Allan Dizioli, Christian Ebeke, Huidan Lin, Linda Kaltani, Sebastian Sosa, Antonio Spilimbergo, and Petia Topalova "The Refugee Surge in Europe: Economic Challenge" (IMF Staff Discussion Noye January 2016)
[20] Daniel Endres, UNHCR's funding in 2015 and requirements in 2016 (65th standing committee, March 15-17 2016)
[21] Oxfam, "The Human Costs of the Funding Shortfalls for the Dadaab Refugee Camps" (2012). https://www.oxfam.org/sites/www.oxfam.org/files/the-human-costs-of-the-funding-shortfalls-for-the-dadaab-refugee-camps.pdf
[22] World Bank, *Forcibly Displaced. Toward a development approach supporting refugees, the internally displaced, and their hosts* ADVANCE EDITION (2015)
[23] Lorena Rios, "How Turkey's Syrian Refugees are Getting By" *al-monitor* (March 28,2016). http://www.al-monitor.com/pulse/originals/2016/03/turkey-syria-refugees-informal-economy-work-permits.html
[24] UNHCR *Global Trends* 2015
[25] UNHCR Statistical Yearbook 2014
[26] UNHCR Statistical Yearbook 2014
[27] UNHCR website, http://www.unhcr.org/pages/49c3646c101.html. Accessed January 11, 2017
[28] UNHCR, *Global Trends 2015*
[29] UNHCR, *Global Trends 2015*
[30] UNHCR, *Global Trends 2015*
[31] UNHCR, Global Trends 2015. Global Trends reports from previous years indicate that in 2014 there were 2.9 million new refugees, 2.5 million in 2013, 1.1 million in 2012 and 0.8 million in 2011.
[38] UNHCR *Asylum Trends 2013.*

[39] Klaus Neumann, Across the Seas. Australia's Response to Refugees. A History. (Black Inc, 2015)
[40] Cited in Klaus Neumann, *Across the Seas. Australia's Response to Refugees* (Black Inc, 2015) p278
[41] Cited in Neumann, *Across the Seas*, p273
[42] G Hand (Minister for Immigration, Local Government and Ethnic Affairs), *Migration Amendment Bill 1992*, Second reading speech, 5 May 1992
[43] Philips and Spinks, "Boat Arrivals in Australia Since 1976", Australian Parliamentary Library, 2013
[44] See Murray, Davidson, Schweizer, "Psychological Wellbeing of Refugees Resettling in Australia. A Literature Review prepared for The Australian Psychological Society", August 2008
[45] Reported in Creswell, "Call to abandon 'factories for mental illness'" *The Australian* Jan 26, 2010
[46] Derrick Silove, Zachary Steel, Richard F Mollica, "Detention of asylum seekers: assault on health, human rights, and social development", Lancet 2001, 357: 1436–37
[47] Kaldor Centre, Temporary Protection Visa Factsheet. Accesed at http://www.kaldorcentre.unsw.edu.au/publication/temporary-protection-visas on January 9, 2017
[48] UNHCR, Asylum Trends 2013. Levels and Trends in Industrialized Countries
[49] Greg Lake, "What Kind of Nation Are We Building?" January 19, 2015 at http://www.asyluminsight.com/c-greg-lake/#.WC83UqJ95uU
[50] Lexi Metherell, "Immigration detention psychiatrist Dr Peter Young says treatment of asylum seekers akin to torture" (6 Aug 2014) http://www.abc.net.au/news/2014-08-05/psychiatrist-says-treatment-of-asylum-seekers-akin-to-torture/5650992
[51] Jane McAdam and Fiona Chong, *Refugees. Why Seeking Asylum is Legal and Australia's Policies Are Not* (UNSW Press, 2015)
[52] A list of the reports can be found at on the Australian Parliament House library website http://www.aph.gov.au/About_Parliament/Parliamentary_Departments/Parliamentary_Library/pubs/rp/rp1516/Quick_Guides/Offshore

[53] Michael Pezzzulio, Senate Estimates, 2016. Found at http://www.border.gov.au/about/news-media/speeches-presentations/secretary-commissioner-joint-statement-17102016
[54] Tara Brian and Frank Laczko (eds), *Fatal Journeys. Tracking Lives Lost During Migration* (IOM 2014)
[55] Malay and Ireland, "Our asylum seeker policy is cruel: Malcolm Turnbull", Sydney Morning Herald, 20 August, 2013, http://www.smh.com.au/federal-politics/federal-election-2013/our-asylum-seeker-policy-is-cruel-malcolm-turnbull-20130819-2s7d7.html#ixzz2w0nj1Zk8
[56] UNHCR Global Resettlement Needs 2017
[57] Government of Canada, UNHCR Resettlement handbook, Canada Country Chapter (July 2011, revised October 2016) p2
[58] Government of Australia, UNHCR Resettlement handbook, Australia Country Chapter (July 2011, revised April 2016) p3
[59] ABS, Prisoners in Australia, 2013
[60] http://theconversation.com/factcheck-qanda-have-any-refugees-who-came-to-australia-gone-on-to-be-terrorists-51192
[61] https://www.theguardian.com/australia-news/datablog/2014/oct/30/australians-think-muslim-population-nine-times-greater
[62] Pew Research Centre, *The Future of World Religions: Population Growth Projections, 2010-2050. Why Muslims Are Rising Fastest and the Unaffiliated Are Shrinking as a Share of the World's Population* (April, 2015)
[63] cited in Australian Muslims. 2015
[64] Dunn, K. M., Atie, R., Mapedzahama, V., Ozalp, M., & Aydogan, A. F. The Resilience and Ordinariness of Australian Muslims: Attitudes and Experiences of Muslims Report. (Penrith, N.S.W.: Western Sydney University. 2015)
[65] Dunn et al Resilience and Ordinariness p39
[66] Department of Social Services, "Settlement Services for Humanitarian Entrants" Sourced at https://www.dss.gov.au/sites/default/files/documents/04_2016/support_for_humanitarian_entrants_0.pdf
[67] http://statisticstimes.com/economy/countries-by-projected-gdp.php
[68] UNHCR, Global Trends 2015
[83] I have been unable to find an original reference for this story.

[84] Mackay, Thomas, and Kneebone, "'It Would be Okay If They Came through the Proper Channels': Community Perceptions and Attitudes toward Asylum Seekers in Australia", *Journal of Refugee Studies*, 2012
[85] Hugh Riminton, Sudan Impact – how a Handshake Can Chsnge Everything, Daily Telegraph, January 6, 2017
[86] "National Interest", http://hass.unsw.adfa.edu.au/timor_companion/fracturing_the_bipartisan_consensus/national_interest.php
[87] Nye, Joseph, "Redefining the National Interest", *Foreign Affairs*, July/August, 1999
[88] The three forms of power are described by Jospeh Nye in "Think Again. Soft Power", *Foreign Policy*, February 23, 2006
[89] Paul Collier, *The Bottom Billion: Why the Poorest Countries are Failing and What Can Be Done About It* (Oxford University Press, 2007)
[90] http://www.unhcr.org/en-au/partners/donors/558a639f9/contributions-unhcr-budget-year-2015-31-december-2015.html
[91] http://www.tradingeconomics.com/australia/government-spending
[92] I have used the World Bank income classification, which identifies high income nations as those with per capita GNI of US$12,476 or more.
[93] Refugee Council of Australia, "Australia's Response To A World In Crisis. Community views on planning for the 2016-17 Refugee and Humanitarian Program" March 2016
[94] See Parsons, Richard, "Assessing the Economic Contribution of Refugees in Australia. A Literature Review". Brisbane: Multicultural Development Association. June 2013
[97] The Expert Panel on Asylum Seekers received advice from the government that it would cost $350 million per year to increase Australia's humanitarian program by 6250 places.
[98] Lisa Button and Shane Evans, *At What Cost? The Human, Economic and Strategic Cost of Australia's Asylum Seeker Policies and the Alternatives* (Save the Children and UNCEF, September 2016)
[99] Button and Evans, *At What Cost?* Pp 42-45
[100] UNHCR Asia Pacific website. http://www.unhcr.org/en-au/asia-and-the-pacific.html. Accessed January 9, 2017

[101] W. Courtland Robinson, "The Comprehensive Plan of Action for Indochinese Refugees, 1989-1997: Sharing the Burden and Passing the Buck", *Journal of Refugee Studies* Vol 17, No 3, 2004

[102] Australian Border Force, "Illegal Maritime Arrivals on Bridging Visa E" September 2016

[113] Clarkson, *History of the Abolition of the Slave Trade, Volume 1,* 1808

www.ingramcontent.com/pod-product-compliance
Lightning Source LLC
Chambersburg PA
CBHW070626300426
44113CB00010B/1680